The
Colorado
14ers
The Best Routes

The East Face of Longs Peak.

THE COLORADO
MOUNTAIN CLUB
GUIDEBOOK

The Colorado 14ers

The Best Routes

THE COLORADO MOUNTAIN CLUB FOUNDATION

The Colorado Mountain Club Press
Golden, Colorado

The Colorado 14ers: The Best Routes
© 2018 by The Colorado Mountain Club Foundation

PUBLISHED BY

The Colorado Mountain Club Press
710 Tenth Street, #200, Golden, Colorado 80401
303-996-2743 | email: cmcpress@cmc.org | www.cmc.org

Founded in 1912, The Colorado Mountain Club is the largest outdoor recreation, education, and conservation organization in the Rocky Mountains. Look for our books at your local bookstore or outdoor retailer or online at www.cmc.org

CORRECTIONS: We greatly appreciate when readers alert us to errors or outdated information by contacting cmcpress@cmc.org.

Takeshi Takahashi: design, composition, and production
Todd Caudle: photographer
Clyde Soles: publisher

Cover/title page: Capitol Peak by Todd Caudle. www.skylinepress.com

DISTRIBUTED TO THE BOOK TRADE BY

Mountaineers Books
1001 SW Klickitat Way, Suite 201, Seattle, WA 98134, 800-553-4453
www.mountaineersbooks.org

TOPOGRAPHIC MAPS are created with CalTopo.com software. Overview map image from NASA/Goddard Space Flight Center Scientific Visualization Studio.

Historical notes adapted from *A Climbing Guide to Colorado's Fourteeners* by Walter R. Borneman and Lyndon J. Lampert.

Printed in Korea

ISBN 978-1-937052-57-7

Contents

An Introduction to the Fourteeners 10

FRONT RANGE

Longs Peak 33
Grays Peak 37
Torreys Peak 37
Mount Evans 41
Mount Bierstadt 45
Pikes Peak 49

SANGRE DE CRISTO RANGE

Kit Carson Peak 53
Challenger Point 53
Humboldt Peak 57
Crestone Peak 61
Crestone Needle 65
Mount Lindsey 69
Little Bear Peak 73
Blanca Peak 77
Ellingwood Point 77
Culebra Peak 81

TENMILE AND MOSQUITO RANGES

Quandary Peak 85
Mount Democrat 89
Mount Cameron 89
Mount Lincoln 89
Mount Bross 89
Mount Sherman 93

SAWATCH RANGE

Mount of the Holy Cross 97
Mount Massive 101
Mount Elbert 105
La Plata Peak 109

Mount Belford.. 113
Mount Oxford.. 113
Missouri Mountain.. 117
Huron Peak... 121
Mount Harvard... 125
Mount Columbia... 125
Mount Yale.. 129
Mount Princeton... 133
Mount Antero... 137
Mount Shavano... 141
Tabeguache Peak.. 141

ELK MOUNTAINS

Capitol Peak.. 145
Snowmass Mountain.. 149
Maroon Peak... 153
North Maroon Peak... 157
Pyramid Peak.. 161
Castle Peak... 165

SAN JUAN MOUNTAINS

San Luis Peak.. 169
Uncompahgre Peak... 173
Wetterhorn Peak.. 177
Redcloud Peak... 181
Sunshine Peak... 181
Handies Peak... 185
Sunlight Peak.. 189
Windom Peak... 189
Mount Eolus.. 193
North Eolus... 193
Mount Sneffels.. 197
Wilson Peak.. 201
Mount Wilson.. 205
El Diente Peak... 209

COLORADO 14ers LOCATOR MAP

FRONT RANGE

		Rank
1	Longs Peak	15
2	Grays Peak	10
3	Torreys Peak	12
4	Mount Evans	14
5	Mount Bierstadt	38
6	Pikes Peak	31

SANGRE DE CRISTO RANGE

7	Kit Carson Peak	23
8	Humboldt Peak	37
9	Crestone Peak	7
10	Crestone Needle	21
11	Mount Lindsey	43
12	Little Bear Peak	44
13	Blanca Peak	4
14	Ellingwood Point	42
15	Culebra Peak	41

TENMILE AND MOSQUITO RANGES

16	Quandary Peak	13
17	Mount Democrat	28
18	Mount Lincoln	8
19	Mount Bross	22
20	Mount Sherman	45

SAWATCH RANGE

21	Mount of the Holy Cross	53
22	Mount Massive	2
23	Mount Elbert	1
24	La Plata Peak	5
25	Mount Belford	19
26	Mount Oxford	26
27	Missouri Mountain	36
28	Huron Peak	52
29	Mount Harvard	3
30	Mount Columbia	35
31	Mount Yale	20
32	Mount Princeton	18
33	Mount Antero	11
34	Mount Shavano	17
35	Tabeguache Peak	25

ELK MOUNTAINS

36	Capitol Peak	30
37	Snowmass Mountain	32
38	Maroon Peak	24
39	North Maroon Peak	48
40	Pyramid Peak	47
41	Castle Peak	9

SAN JUAN MOUNTAINS

42	San Luis Peak	51
43	Uncompahgre Peak	6
44	Wetterhorn Peak	50
45	Redcloud Peak	46
46	Sunshine Peak	54
47	Handies Peak	40
48	Sunlight Peak	39
49	Windom Peak	34
50	Mount Eolus	33
51	Mount Sneffels	29
52	Wilson Peak	49
53	Mount Wilson	16
54	El Diente Peak	27

An Introduction to the Fourteeners

If you are considering climbing a Fourteener for the first time, we suggest that you select a moderate route. Note that there is no such thing as an "easy" Fourteener. Many of these peaks have multiple options for hiking or scrambling to the summit, and the routes that are considered "best" are usually the easiest. The more serious among us call them "trade routes," because they get so much traffic. That also means they have the best maintained trails.

The climbs in this book are recommended by the Colorado Fourteeners Initiative (CFI) and the US Forest Service (USFS) as the most sustainable routes that do the least environmental damage. "Wait," you're thinking. "How can a climber cause environmental damage?" In general, it's not about you, because you stay on durable surfaces like rock and snow, you don't walk beside a trail because it's muddy, and you don't shortcut switchbacks because it's faster. It's much more about the carrying capacity of these high-altitude trails and the fact that more than 300,000 people per summer attempt at least one Fourteener. In addition, many of these trails are braided and the multiple paths all headed generally in the same direction tend to erode during spring runoff and summer thunderstorms. And it should be obvious that many of the plants that grow at altitude don't do well when repeatedly stomped.

Additionally, if you are a climber who is new to the Fourteeners, there is some basic stuff that you should understand before attempting any of the routes, such as acclimatization, hydration, nutrition, and being off the summit by noon. Our sidebars talk about this basic information, and we encourage you to read all of them. We also recommend that you to get a recent edition of *Mountaineering: The Freedom of the Hills* from Mountaineers Books and read and understand the first four or five chapters.

This book is intended as an easy reference to the mountains that you haven't climbed. Use it as a primer on the Fourteeners and you will most likely have enjoyable and succesful adventures to their summits. But we also understand that you may be looking for greater challenges or details than provided here. For more detailed information, we recommend Gerry Roach's *Colorado's Fourteeners*, and for the latest conditions, go to Bill Middlebrook's *14ers.com*.

Wetterhorn Peak.

HISTORY

The Fourteeners stretch across Colorado from Longs Peak in the Front Range, in sight of Wyoming; to Culebra Peak, just north of New Mexico; to the San Juan Range near the famous Four Corners area, where Colorado, Arizona, New Mexico, and Utah meet. Climbing the Fourteeners will take you to many parts of Colorado and will introduce you to a variety of flora, fauna, and rock, and even a little history.

An arrowhead found on the boulder field below the summit of Longs Peak and a man-made shelter discovered at the apex of Blanca yield evidence that Native Americans did climb Colorado's great mountains.

Members of several early expeditions, especially the Hayden and Wheeler Surveys, climbed many of the Fourteeners. A survey team

Handies Peak.

climbed and named Mount Harvard and Mount Yale in 1869, while Mount Massive and Mount Elbert were summited in 1874.

Trappers and miners also climbed some of the great mountains, and prospect holes were found near the summits of Handies Peak and Mount Bierstadt, while abandoned cabins and mines dot the flanks of Mount Democrat and Mount Lincoln. Early climbers discovered evidence that grizzly bears may have used the summits of several peaks as habitat. A she-grizzly "came rushing past us," reported a climber nearing the summit of Uncompahgre Peak in 1874, and claw marks were discovered on the rock near the summit of Mount Sneffels.

The first record of someone climbing all of the then-known Fourteeners in Colorado dates to 1923, when Carl Blaurock and William Ervin achieved this feat. In 1912, Blaurock was one of the charter members of The Colorado Mountain Club (CMC), whose history is intimately tied to the exploration, mapping, and even naming of Colorado's mountains.

COUNTING FOURTEENERS

How many Fourteeners are there? That question has intrigued climbers since the early days of exploration. A guide published in 1925 lists 47. Included in this ranking are Stewart Peak in the San Juan Range and Grizzly Peak in the Sawatch Range, which later were demoted to Thirteeners. Missouri Mountain and its neighbor, Huron Peak, were added to the list in the mid-1950s after new measurements. Mount of the Holy Cross appeared on the list, was taken off, and then reinstated. At some point, both Mount Hope and Ice Mountain were called Fourteeners, though they are well below the requisite altitude.

Today, 54 mountains are recognized as Fourteeners by the CMC—those are the peaks you are supposed to climb to make the annual list of summiters (*CMC.org/MySummits/SummitCompletionForm.aspx*). However, depending upon whom you ask, the count ranges between 52 and 59 (or even 76). The reasons for the discrepancy are differing definitions of a "Fourteener" and improvements in mapping technology.

The most common definition requires that a Fourteener must rise 300 feet above the saddle connecting it to the nearest Fourteener. Sticking strictly to that rule, at the moment, there are 53 Fourteeners. However, the CMC includes two peaks—El Diente (239 feet prominence) and North Maroon (234 feet prominence)—because of their challenge and beauty. And the CMC leaves off Challenger Point, which is more of a hump on the ridge leading to Kit Carson Peak than a worthy climb of its own (the height of the saddle is also in question since it hasn't been surveyed accurately and only makes the cut by 2 feet). So 53 + 2 − 1 = 54 Fourteeners.

The Colorado Geological Survey recognizes 58 named peaks over 14,000 feet. In addition to the ones above, these include Mount Cameron (138 feet prominence), Conundrum Peak (240 feet prominence), and North Eolus (179 feet prominence). As with Challenger Point, the CMC doesn't consider these "true Fourteeners" because these aren't peaks worth a climb all by themselves.

The so-called 59th Fourteener—Sunlight Spire (228 feet prominence)—isn't named on a USGS map and was only updated to 14,001 feet in 1991 based upon a change in the sea-level standard. If it were an official Fourteener, this would be the most difficult in the Lower 48 States, including the 12 (or 15) in California and 2 in Washington.

If you count every unnamed peak above 14,000 feet, with a minimum of 40 feet of prominence, that brings the total to 73 Fourteeners (or 74 if you include that pesky Sunlight Spire) according to our friend Gerry Roach. You won't see these names on a USGS map but he calls them: North Massive, Massive Green, East Crestone, West Evans, Northeast Crestone, East La Plata, South Elbert, South Massive, South Wilson, West Wilson, Southeast Longs, South Bross, South Little Bear, Northwest Lindsey, and North Snowmass (plus two weird highpoints).

As mentioned, there are 53 Fourteeners following the "Colorado rule" based on a minimum of 300 feet of rise from the connecting saddle to next Fourteener. But if you follow the Alaska rule, which requires 3,000 feet of prominence, there are only 10 Fourteeners in Colorado. Or, if you follow the Washington rule with 400 feet of prominence...oh, never mind.

So that settles it, right? Not so fast. In the United States, peaks are measured by the National Geodetic Survey (NGS), a division of the National Oceanic and Atmospheric Administration (NOAA) and they are mapped and named by the United States Geological Survey (USGS). The NGS establishes the vertical datum, which is essentially the baseline for sea level. [Here you can dive into fun topics like "geoid," "mean sea level," and "equipotential gravitational surface."] Considering that sea level varies by about 30 feet around North America, the chosen point, currently a lighthouse in Quebec, can make or break a lot of Fourteeners and other bragging rights.

Many of the USGS maps were created using the National Geodetic Vertical Datum of 1929 (NGVD29) and printed peak height is based on that information. However, the NGS released a more accurate set of data in 1991 called the North America Vertical Datum of 1988 (NAVD88) and many peaks in Colorado suddenly "grew" a few feet. This is the system used by GPS receivers and smartphones, though many printed maps still list older elevations.

With the datum change, 28 named Fourteeners increased their elevation; most of these grew about 6 feet. Castle Peak was the big winner by growing 14 feet taller and moving from 12th to 9th highest peak in the state. El Diente stayed the same height but dropped from 24th to 28th highest.

Sunlight Peak.

Okay, fine. All peak elevations are now based on NAVD88, so we're done, right? Not quite. The NGS is working on a new datum that will be released in 2022. This data set will be based upon extremely accurate gravity measurements from instruments mounted in planes that are resurveying the entire country.

Though the results aren't final, the early indications are that much of Colorado will drop about 2 feet. Which means that Sunshine Peak will soon be off the list (sorry, building a big rock pile doesn't count). And the nefarious Sunlight Spire won't be pestering Fourteener summiters.

Given all that, CMC is sticking with our list of 54 Fourteeners to receive an achievement certificate. You can climb the 58, or 59, or whatever. Many people that far in the game move on to climbing the Centennials—the highest 100 peaks in the Centennial State (aka Colorado). Which leads them to climbing all 584 Thirteeners. And for the really obsessed, ascend the 676 Twelvers (so far, only 7 people have climbed all 1,313 peaks over 12,000 feet). Don't forget the 64 county highpoints. The CMC keeps lists of finishers for most of them and is happy to document your passion!

FOURTEENER RECORDS

There are countless records involving Fourteeners. Although impressive feats, the CMC does not officially track fast ascents and linkups. Nor does the Club track youngest/oldest, dog ascents (illegal on some peaks and dangerous on others), or even the position on the list of Fourteener Finishers (changes as more information comes in). For speed records, a good information source is *FastestKnownTime.com*.

It can be difficult to compare some of the records because of different peak lists and routes. Some years, Culebra, Democrat, and Lincoln have been closed to the public. Those pursuing records are supposed to follow the "Colorado Rule," which mandates 3,000 feet of ascent and descent along with a plethora of other requirements.

The quest for speed started in 1960 when Cleve McCarty climbed 52 Fourteeners (the tally at the time) in 52 days. The Smith family cut this time to 33 days for 54 peaks in 1974 and it was down to 17 days by 1990.

All of the early speed ascents were self-supported, relying on no outside help except perhaps car shuttles on traverses. These days, the trend is for sponsored athletes attempting Fastest Known Times (FKT) on absurdly hard and/or long routes in wilderness areas. They often have a support team staged along the course and pacers running with them.

At present, Andrew Hamilton holds the fastest time for climbing 58 Fourteeners: an incredible 9 days and 21 hours, covering 265 miles with

Mount Sneffels.

140,000 feet of ascent and descent. His son, Axel, is probably the youngest to climb the Fourteeners after finishing them all in 2016 at age 6. The female record holder for climbing the 54 Fourteeners is Danelle Ballengee who finished in 14 days and 15 hours.

Another style of speed ascents is self-powered by bike. In 1985, Glen and Pete Dunmire climbed 54 Fourteeners in 61 days while carrying all their supplies on bikes. In 2016, Joe Grant climbed 58 Fourteeners by cycling over 1,400 miles in just 31 days and 9 hours.

The "purest" style of climbing the Fourteeners is entirely on foot. In 1985, Patrick Renworth and Mike Whitehurst took about 120 days to walk 1,600 miles while climbing 54 Fourteeners. The current fastest thru-hike for 58 Fourteeners is held by Junaid Dawud and Luke DeMuth, who covered 1,300 miles and 300,000 feet of elevation gain in 72 days.

It took 13 years but in 1991 Lou Dawson became the first person to ski from the summit of all 54 Fourteeners. In 2006, Chris Davenport skied them all in 363 days and totaled about 200,000 feet of climbing. The new record, established in 2017, belongs to Josh Jespersen, who completed the descents in 138 days.

Another test of lung and muscle power is known as the "Nolan's 14," which is a traverse of the Sawatch Range (in either direction) over 14 Fourteeners. Devised by Jim Nolan in 1991, this is a roughly 100-mile challenge (without a specified course) between Mounts Massive and Shavano, nearly all above timberline, with about 44,000 feet of climbing and a time limit of 60 hours. Considered one of the hardest ultrarun challenges in the country, it was first completed in 2001 and just two dozen people have finished so far. The current record belongs to Iker Karrera, who ran his course in 48 hours and 40 minutes.

Many of the Fourteeners have been climbed in astounding times. But since routes and start/finish points vary, comparisons are difficult. Only Pikes Peak has an official trail race with accurate timing; in 1993, Matt Carpenter completed the round-trip marathon (26.2 miles) in 3 hours

Mount of the Holy Cross.

and 17 minutes. In 2012, famed ultrarunner Anton Krupicka climbed and descended Longs Peak via the Keyhole Route in 3 hours and 15 minutes. A couple weeks later, he did the round-trip on Grays and Torreys in 1 hour and 31 minutes.

There are also all sorts of oddball records to pursue such as the "Longs Peak Triathlon," an unofficial challenge started in 1974 that involves riding a bike from Boulder to Longs Peak, running and climbing the route of choice, running down, then cycling back to Boulder. Depending on the route, it's about 75 miles of cycling and 15 miles of running, possibly with some serious climbing, and 11,500 feet of elevation gain. The current FKT is under 10 hours and it's been done entirely on foot in 29 hours.

HOW TO USE THIS GUIDEBOOK

The peaks are grouped by the ranges in which they are found, and the ranges are listed from east to west across Colorado. Within each range the peaks are cited from north to south.

The information on **MAPS** at the top of each description includes the Trails Illustrated map that you will need to do the route. Of course there are numerous ways to access digital maps but it's wise to have backup in case electronics fail.

The routes shown on the maps in this book are based on the GPS readings taken by the Colorado Fourteeners Initiative in 2017. These are more accurate than the trails printed on most maps, reflecting the latest trail locations. However, some of these trails will inevitably be rerouted to lessen environmental impact so stay alert. Remember that route finding is part of the adventure, and that if the route gets real difficult quickly, you are probably off-route and need to back up.

The climbers who have shared their knowledge of the Colorado Fourteeners and suggested **RATINGS** in this book maintain that there really are no "easy" high-altitude mountains. Slippery cliffs, falling rock, crumbling ledges, heaving talus slopes, and abrupt changes in the weather can turn a pleasant hike into a difficult climb. Thus, none of the mountains is rated as "easy." Our ratings are "Moderate," "More difficult," and "Very difficult," all relative terms depending on weather, the climber's physical condition, and the time of the year. We do make a point, however, of telling you if a mountain is more strenuous or time-consuming and if the climb can be particularly dangerous.

ELEVATION GAINS are self-explanatory. Where two peaks are traditionally climbed in one day, the elevation gain and **ROUND-TRIP DISTANCE** are recorded for doing both mountains. The approximate elevation gains depend on where you start or where you camp. Note that on some of these routes there is a substantial loss of altitude on the approach, which can mean a nasty climb at the end of a long day.

The estimated **ROUND-TRIP DISTANCE** and particularly the **ROUND-TRIP TIME** are just that: estimates. The **NEAREST TOWN** is a recognizable town on a Colorado state road map. We've also included the **RANGER DISTRICT** in which each route is located, or contact information if the land is privately owned.

Descriptions start out with a **COMMENT**. These comments typically note mountains that are done together, difficult routes that require traditional climbing gear, objective dangers, mountains with roads to the top, and the name of the standard route.

GETTING THERE is a section that describes how to get to the trailhead and, often, where to park once you are there. Some of these routes require four-wheel-drive vehicles with good clearance. We are not kidding about gnarly roads. The locals are vastly entertained when they come upon a rental subcompact on its side. And if you rent a vehicle at Denver International Airport, be careful; driving these roads is a little trickier than you might imagine, particularly when they are wet.

The **ROUTES** described here are for summer and early autumn trips. Winter conditions can alter not only the route but also the entire climbing experience.

CLIMBING THE FOURTEENERS

When you consider climbing a Fourteener, the words challenge, fun, and adventure all come to mind. Indeed, those of us involved in producing this book have felt and enjoyed all of that and more in the High Country. But we also ask you to be serious and keep in mind such words as: danger, disaster, and pain. If you are sick, hurt, or disabled on any of the high peaks, getting down can be problematic. Our friends in mountain rescue groups, county sheriff's departments, and federal agencies have risked a great deal over the years to bring broken or lifeless bodies down from the Fourteeners. Don't let that be you.

Here are some truths about climbing Colorado's highest mountains:

Mount Yale.

Route descriptions cannot be relied upon as a substitute for good judgment and careful preparation. No guidebook can make provisions for the many variables that affect a climb, such as weather, the physical condition of the participants, and the possibility that climbers will fail to locate the described landmarks.

High mountains are subject to abrupt and drastic weather changes. Lightning storms should always be expected when climbing the Fourteeners from April to September, and some peaks do seem to have more storms than others. Due to the frequency of early afternoon storms, summer climbs should be planned so that the party is descending from the summit by noon. Consult SummitCAST (*bouldercast.com/summitcast-hiking-forecast/*) for excellent mountain-specific forecasts.

Breathing almost three miles above sea level and climbing several miles upwards will tire you quickly. The more serious physical discomforts high-altitude climbers may encounter are nausea, headache, and, occasionally, heart palpitations, and disorientation.

There are inherent risks in climbing mountains and it is incumbent upon everyone to know them. High altitude often means low temperatures and very strong winds. Hence, frostbite and hypothermia are possible dangers. You can become exhausted or lost, or you may find yourself facing cliffs that require technical rock-climbing skills. The consequences of climbing beyond your ability can be severe; you not only expose yourself to injury but also endanger those hiking with you or coming to your assistance.

We climb to challenge the limits of our bodies and our wills, and to test our capacity for risks. Yet, to go unprepared—to carry no maps or compass, to take an inadequate amount of water, or to eschew a pack with warm clothing and rain gear—is simply dumb. On a Fourteener, a cloudless, sunny day can rapidly change to a snowstorm or a whiteout, drinking unpurified stream water can expose you to waterborne parasites, and a lightning strike can ruin your day.

If all that makes climbing Fourteeners seem too daunting, the CMC offers a wide variety of classes to help you prepare. In addition, we have hundreds of group hikes around the state to help you gain experience with like-minded people.

ACCESS TO THE FOURTEENERS

As of 2018, there is no access to the summit of Mount Bross. Access to Culebra Peak is limited and on a fee basis. Check with the Colorado Fourteeners Initiative (*14ers.org*) for up-to-date information.

On a number of Fourteener routes, you will be passing near or over private property. This access, if abused in any way, can and has been denied over the years. Be an adult and act responsibly. Tread lightly on private property and treat it and the owners with respect.

SIDEBAR / **BOOTS**

It should go without saying that the boots you use on a Fourteener must be broken in. We have used everything from heavy leather mountaineering boots to trail running shoes. The old waffle-stompers were just too heavy. The trail running shoes were ultralight, but offered no protection at all. We now compromise with high-topped, lightweight hiking boots made out of few discernable natural materials. These boots are light and tough, and they offer some protection, provide decent support, and have an aggressive tread pattern.

THE 10 ESSENTIALS

A properly equipped hiker will more likely than not have a successful outing. Essential equipment includes: broken-in hiking boots over wool socks on your feet and an extra pair of socks in your pack; quick-drying pants or rain pants, not cotton jeans; a lightweight wool or synthetic shirt, not cotton; a hooded waterproof jacket; a warm head covering and gloves; and plenty of water, plus at least one meal and additional snacks.

All hikers and mountain climbers should carry in their daypacks or backpacks the following:

1. Navigation (real map and compass)
2. Headlamp
3. Hydration
4. Nutrition
5. Sun hat, sunglasses, sunscreen
6. Insulation
7. First aid
8. Repair kit
9. Fire
10. Shelter

Uncompahgre Peak.

Castle Peak.

You need this stuff to survive the worst that the high mountains can hand out. If you cannot carry the extra weight, perhaps you should reconsider your decision to climb a Fourteener in the first place. Some of the peaks may require the use of a helmet, a rope, and occasionally, an ice axe. Climbers attempting these mountains should be familiar with belay and self-arrest techniques. It is also imperative that you tell a family member or friend where you are going and when you expect to return. And don't forget to sign in at the trailhead if a register is available.

CMC FOURTEENER REGISTERS

The CMC began placing registers on the peaks of the Fourteeners in the 1910s and 1920s. Old registers, which are available to researchers, are archived at the American Mountaineering Center in Golden, Colorado. Registers from the early years of the 20th century show that the number of climbers scaling the Fourteeners remained fairly constant until the 1950s. Climbing increased in popularity in the 1960s and 1970s, and exploded in the 1980s and 1990s. On a popular mountain such as Longs Peak, a register with room for 500 names fills in a week.

Registers are rolled up and stored in PVC plastic canisters secured at the summit by a cable or rock. Sometimes it is difficult to find the small, inconspicuous gray tube. Once you locate the canister, sign your name with a ballpoint pen or with a pencil. Signatures made with other sorts of pens tend to bleed on the entire register and obliterate names.

The CMC maintains a list of those who have climbed all of the Fourteeners and registered their accomplishment. At the end of 2017, the list contained 1,809 names. Climbers who have completed all 54 Fourteeners are encouraged to register their accomplishment at *CMC.org/MySummits/SummitCompletionForm.aspx* to be included in the CMC's annual listing and receive a certificate.

THE COLORADO MOUNTAIN CLUB FOUNDATION

The Colorado Mountain Club Foundation (CMCF) was incorporated in 1973 as a 501(c)(3) non-profit organization. The Foundation receives, administers, and disburses funds for tax-exempt charitable, scientific, literary, and educational purposes. Since 1981, the CMCF has given grants to students in college and graduate school doing research in history, geology, geography, biology, and other aspects of Colorado's mountains. In 2017, the CMCF delivered over $12,000 in fellowship awards to ten students.

The CMCF has also provided loans to the Wilderness Land Trust to permit the purchase of land when it becomes available in areas where trail access is restricted. The Gehres Fourteeners Fund maintained by the CMCF is dedicated to protecting Colorado's high peaks from encroachment and damage due to overuse, protecting public access, and providing public education with regard to conservation, preservation, and sanitation.

In addition, the CMCF publishes brochures to educate hikers on hypothermia, lightning, and snow avalanches, and distributes these materials free of charge to hikers through the CMC, the Forest Service, the National Park Service, and outdoor retailers.

Individuals active in the CMCF volunteer their time and contributions to the CMCF are tax deductible. Royalties from this guidebook will benefit the work of the CMCF. Learn more about the organization at *cmcfoundation.net.*

COLORADO FOURTEENERS INITIATIVE

In 1994, the Colorado Fourteeners Initiative (CFI) was founded by the Colorado Mountain Club, Colorado Outward Bound School, Volunteers for Outdoor Colorado, Rocky Mountain Field Institute, Leave No Trace Center for Outdoor Ethics, and the US Forest Service. Since then, the CFI has become the nation's leading organization building sustainable trails at high altitudes, restoring damaged tundra, and providing on-moun-

Mount Massive.

Mount Lincoln.

tain education to Fourteener climbers. CFI's projects do not make the Fourteeners any easier to climb, but they protect these unique natural resources from harm to ensure the long-term sustainability of recreation on these peaks.

Colorado's Fourteeners are magnets for climbers worldwide due to their rugged beauty, varied terrain, and relative ease of access. In 2016, the CFI estimates 311,000 person days of hiking use, a number that grows each year. Increased use combined with poorly located trails has resulted in growing environmental impacts on the fragile alpine tundra on these high peaks. Repeated trampling by climbers kills native plants and harms animal habitat—including some plants and animals that exist nowhere else—threatening ecosystems that took millennia to develop.

To date, CFI has constructed 31 sustainably designed, durably built summit trails on 28 Fourteeners. CFI has engaged almost 13,500 days of volunteer stewardship since 2001 in the construction and maintenance of these peaks. A multi-pronged educational strategy has contacted more than 112,000 hikers in the field through paid crews and volunteer Peak Stewards. Visit their web site at *14ers.org* for more information and the latest trail updates. A portion of the royalties from this book goes to the CFI.

ROCKY MOUNTAIN FIELD INSTITUTE

Founded in 1982, the organization now known as the Rocky Mountain Field Institute (RMFI) has worked to maintain climbing areas in Colorado and Utah. While the CFI maintains trails on the majority of Colorado's Fourteeners, the RMFI works on trails in the Sangre de Cristo Range as well as Pikes Peak and other trails in the Colorado Springs region. Learn more at *RMFI.org.*

LEAVE NO TRACE

The Fourteeners are a harsh, yet fragile, environment. Above timberline, plants grow very slowly due to the harsh conditions and short growing seasons. Even slight disturbances can cause long-term damage. Impacted areas may take hundreds of years to recover.

To minimize environmental impact, hikers should remain on the trail—especially in areas where trail modifications have been made to reduce human impacts. Because of the increased popularity of climbing the Fourteeners, ascents on weekdays not only minimize human impacts but also offer solitude and diminish trail and campground congestion.

The Colorado Fourteeners Initiative has developed these Leave No Trace guidelines that are specific to hiking and climbing the Fourteeners.

Mount Eolus (left), Sunlight Peak (center), and Windom Peak (right).

Culebra Peak.

When hiking on a trail:
- Stay on existing routes and never cut across switchbacks.
- Walk through muddy or snow-covered segments of the trail, not around them.
- When encountering braided or parallel trails, use the most impacted or eroded trail.

When a trail does not exist:
- Travel on durable surfaces such as rock, snow and ridges, and avoid gullies or steep and loose slopes, because these are prone to erosion and alpine vegetation loss.
- Disperse over a wide area if traveling in a group to minimize the impact of stepping on fragile tundra.

When camping in alpine basins:
- Use existing campsites.
- Do not camp above timberline.

Mount Democrat.

FINAL NOTE

In this introduction, and throughout the guidebook, we have talked about safety until you are tired of reading it and begin to think that maybe we are taking ourselves a little too seriously—after all, most of these routes are basically walk-ups. Talk to any mountain rescuer and she or he can tell you 100 different ways to get killed in the mountains, but over the years the big killer has been a slip or fall on rock, snow, or ice. Check out the statistics in the back of any edition of *Accidents in North American Climbing* from the American Alpine Club. The CMC's *Colorado 14er Disasters*, by Mark Scott-Nash, also makes for educational yet sobering reading.

One more thought about climbing, or for that matter, any endeavor that takes you in harm's way: You often get hurt or killed not by one big thing, but by a lot of little things that go wrong. You wake up with a headache. Two miles out of camp you remember that you left your rain jacket in the tent. You get off-route and find yourself in an ugly couloir filled with loose rock, and then it starts to cloud over early. You are looking at a lot of mistakes in a row, some of them your fault. What makes you think you'll stop making mistakes? Turn around, carefully retrace your steps, and get off the mountain. It's not your day.

The mountain will be there forever. Live to try again.

North Maroon and Maroon Peaks.

Longs Peak and Chasm Lake at sunrise.

Longs Peak

14,259 feet **15**

MAPS	Trails Illustrated 301–Longs Peak
RATING	Very difficult
ELEVATION GAIN	5,100 feet
ROUND-TRIP DISTANCE	14.5 miles
ROUND-TRIP TIME	10 to 15 hours
NEAREST TOWN	Estes Park
HEADQUARTERS	National Park Service, Rocky Mountain National Park, 970-586-1206 or *nps.gov/romo*

COMMENT: Plan on a very early start and a very long day. This is the only Colorado Fourteener in a national park. Remember that national park rules apply. The standard route is called the Keyhole Route. The route is rated Very Difficult because most climbers complete the route in one long day.

GETTING THERE: From the intersection of CO 72, follow CO 6 north for 10 miles. From Estes Park, drive south 9 miles on CO 7. Turn west on the road to Longs Peak Ranger station. A left fork leads to the station and parking lot, which is often crowded. The right fork leads to the Longs Peak Campground, where sites are available on a first-come basis. Additional camping is available at backcountry sites, where permits are required. Contact the Backcountry Office (970-586-1242) for information.

THE ROUTE: The trailhead for Longs is next to the ranger station. Follow a good, moderately steep trail 5 miles west to the Boulder Field at about 12,800 feet. Continue southwest for about 1 mile to the Keyhole at 13,100 feet. From here, the route is well marked with yellow and red bull's-eye (otherwise known as fried eggs). Follow the route onto the ledges along the west side of the peak, up the rock trough to the ledge junction, or spur. Turn southeast through the "Narrows" to the "Homestretch" of slab rock. Then continue to the large, flat summit. This is a long, tedious climb—much of it above timberline. There is exposure on the ledges, and the upper mountain can be dangerously slick with ice. Before starting, check with the ranger regarding conditions. At certain times, an ice axe may be needed.

A view of The Diamond from the east.

HISTORY: The Arapaho Indians called Longs Peak and Mount Meeker *Neniis-ótoyóú-'u*, which means the "Two Guides." In 1820, Major Stephen H. Long led an expedition along Colorado's Front Range, and his name soon became associated with this prominent landmark. On August 23, 1868, a party led by John Wesley Powell finally reached the summit, although Arapaho who were trapping eagles may have preceded this first documented ascent.

Longs Peak from Rock Cut, along Trail Ridge Road in Rocky Mountain National Park.

LONGS PEAK

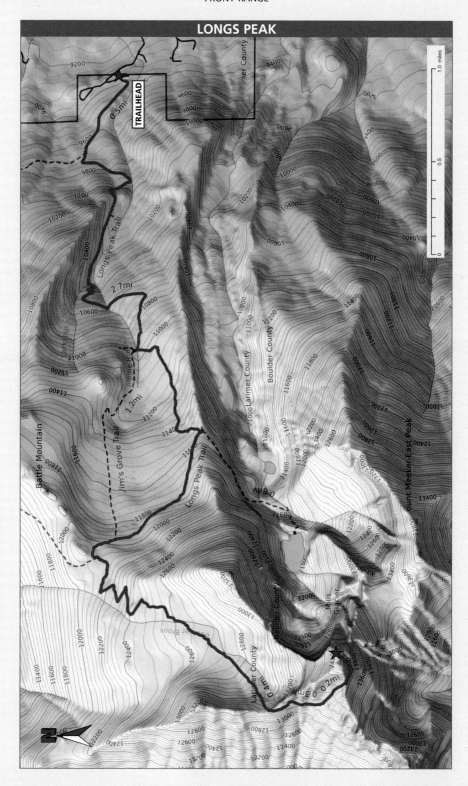

Grays Peak
Torreys Peak

14,278 feet `10`

14,275 feet `12`

MAPS	Trails Illustrated 104–Idaho Springs/Georgetown/Loveland Pass
RATING	Moderate
ELEVATION GAIN	3,000 to 3,600 feet
ROUND-TRIP DISTANCE	8 to 9 miles
ROUND-TRIP TIME	6 to 8 hours
NEAREST TOWN	Silver Plume
RANGER DISTRICT	US Forest Service, Clear Creek Ranger District, 303-567-3000

COMMENT: These two peaks can be climbed in one day with little more effort than it takes to climb only one. Weather, of course, can be a factor in deciding whether to attempt both peaks. Ascending Stevens Gulch to the North Slopes is the standard route. Grays, the peak to the south (left), is usually climbed first. After summiting Grays, you then proceed to the saddle between Grays and Torreys, and climb Torreys. Climbers starting early can drive from Denver and return to the city that same evening.

CFI completed trail construction and restoration work in 2002, and now maintains annually with volunteers and their Adopt-a-Peak Program. CFI plans to begin a focused trail reconstruction and restoration effort here in 2019.

GETTING THERE: From Denver, drive west on Interstate 70 to Bakerville, Exit 221. Turn left over the interstate and drive south 3.5 miles on a steep, but wide and passable, dirt road to the vicinity of Stevens Mine at 11,300 feet. There is a parking lot for about 30 vehicles, and outhouses are adjacent to the parking lot.

THE ROUTE: Take the iron bridge across the stream and follow a good trail that switchbacks for 3.5 miles. At about 13,200 feet, there is a trail junction left and up to Grays. The climber has the choice of continuing up another 0.5 mile to the summit of Grays, or taking the trail west to the saddle between Grays and Torreys at 13,700 feet and climbing Torreys' ridge to the summit.

Left: Torreys Peak (left) and Grays Peak from the south.

After climbing Grays, descend from the summit northwest 600 feet into the saddle on a marked trail and follow the ridge north for 0.5 mile to the summit of Torreys. The distance between the peaks is about 0.7 mile as the crow flies. There is usually an extensive snowfield at the saddle in the spring and early summer. Cross the saddle by post-holing. Try to remain on the trail to avoid trampling on the fragile vegetation on the edges of the snowfield. Proceed with caution.

HISTORY: The Arapaho Indians called Grays and Torreys *Heenii-yoowuu*, meaning the "Anthills." These are the only Fourteeners to sit on the Continental Divide. Botanist Charles Parry, who made the first recorded ascent in 1861, named the peaks for his mentors at Harvard, Asa Gray and John Torrey. Gray climbed the peak in 1872 with his wife in 1872 and again in 1877.

From Torreys, return to the saddle, then work back to the trail down the north side of Grays. Early in the season, this route may entail a climb well up Grays' slope to avoid the usual snow cornice. You may see mountain goats during the climb.

Grays Peak (left) and Torreys Peak (right) from the northeast, viewed from McClellan Mountain.

GRAYS PEAK / TORREYS PEAK

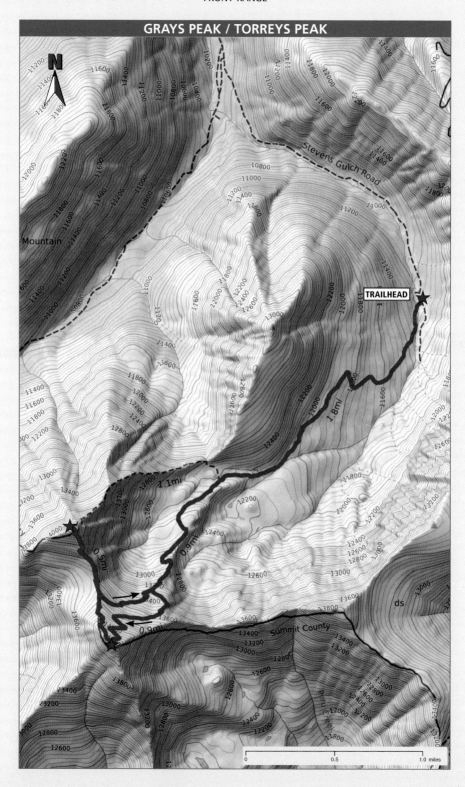

Stevens Gulch Road

TRAILHEAD

Mountain

1.8mi

1.1mi

0.9mi

0.5mi

0.9mi

Summit County

ds

0   0.5   1.0 miles

Mount Evans from the start of Mount Spalding's east ridge.

Mount Evans

14,261 feet 14

MAPS	Trails Illustrated 104–Idaho Springs/Georgetown/Loveland Pass
RATING	Moderate
ELEVATION GAIN	1,400 feet from Summit Lake
ROUND-TRIP DISTANCE	5 miles from Summit Lake
ROUND-TRIP TIME	4 hours from Summit Lake
NEAREST TOWN	Georgetown
RANGER DISTRICT	US Forest Service, Clear Creek Ranger District, 303-567-3000

COMMENT: Mount Evans has a paved toll road to the top that can be run or cycled, but watch out for the traffic. Since there is a paved road to the summit, there is no register. The standard route described here starts at Summit Lake and goes over Mount Spalding to the West Ridge. If you are following the unofficial "3,000-foot Rule" or just don't want pay the $5 fee for the toll road, you can start your hike at Echo Lake and follow the Chicago Lakes Trail to Summit Lake; this adds 3,600 feet of elevation gain and 12 miles. Either climb can be done in a day trip from Denver.

CFI completed trail construction and restoration work on this route in 2006, and now maintains annually with volunteers and their Adopt-a-Peak Program.

GETTING THERE: Take Interstate 70 west to Idaho Springs. Take Exit 240 and follow the signs to Mount Evans Road. Park at the Summit Lake Trailhead if there is space available. Get to Chicago Lakes from the Echo Lake Trailhead near the Echo Lake Lodge.

THE ROUTE: Start from Summit Lake by hiking northwest around the lake to the start of the established trail up the ridge to Mount Spalding. From Spalding, follow the trail along the ridge to the summit of Mount Evans. Note: From Summit Lake, you will not gain the required 3,000 feet in altitude. The Colorado Fourteeners Initiative has built a route from Chicago Lakes basin to Summit Lake that provides hikers with a route that will give them the 3,000 feet of elevation gain. You may see mountain goats during the climb, especially below Summit Lake or on the Sawtooth Ridge between Mount Evans and Mount Bierstadt.

Mount Evans' reflection in Summit Lake.

The view north from Mount Evans' summit.

HISTORY: Once called "Mount Rosalie," the Colorado legislature renamed this peak "Mount Evans" in 1895 in honor of Colorado's second territorial governor. In addition to leadership roles with the Denver Pacific and the Denver, South Park, and Pacific Railroads, John Evans was a benefactor of the University of Denver and an influential businessman.

Mount Evans' east ridge at sunrise.

SIDEBAR

RIDE A FOURTEENER

Held each year in mid-July, the Bob Cook Memorial Mount Evans Hill Climb is a bike race that starts in Idaho Springs at 7,540 feet and climbs on the highest paved road in the United States to the Mount Evans summit over a 27.4-mile route. Tom Danielson holds the record of 1 hour and 41 minutes.

MOUNT EVANS

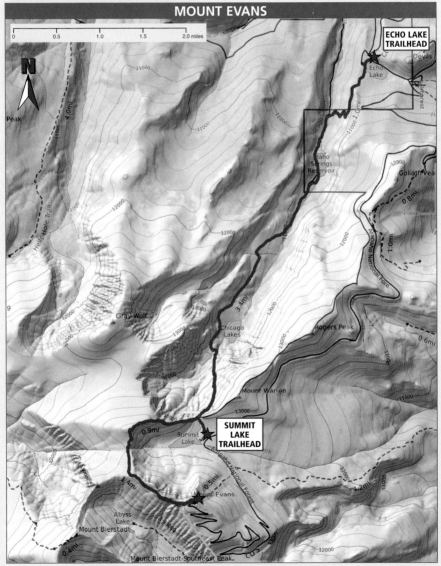

Mount Bierstadt 14,060 feet 38

MAPS	Trails Illustrated 104–Idaho Springs/Georgetown/Loveland Pass
RATING	Moderate
ELEVATION GAIN	2,850 feet
ROUND-TRIP DISTANCE	7 miles
ROUND-TRIP TIME	6 hours
NEAREST TOWN	Georgetown
RANGER DISTRICT	US Forest Service, South Platte Ranger District, 303-275-5610

COMMENT: The standard route starts at the Guanella Pass Trailhead and goes up the West Slopes. Both Mount Bierstadt and Mount Evans may be climbed in one day. However, the Sawtooth Ridge connecting the two mountains is exposed and is difficult if you are not a rock climber. Do not attempt this route unless you are confident of your abilities. If you plan to do this traverse, consult **The Best Denver Hikes** for a description titled "The Tour d'Abyss." Be especially watchful of the weather.

CFI completed trail construction and restoration work on the lower portion of the West Slopes route in 2002. CFI completed trail reconstruction on the upper half of the mountain in 2015, and now maintains annually with volunteers through their Adopt-a-Peak program.

GETTING THERE: From Georgetown, drive south 11 miles along Guanella Pass Scenic Byway (South Clear Creek Road) to Guanella Pass at 11,669 feet. The peak is in view to the east-southeast.

THE ROUTE: Hike 1 mile on trail and boardwalk through the dreaded willows. The trail continues east, then south, to reach the west ridge of the peak. The trail then follows the ridge northeast to the summit.

Left: Mount Bierstadt from Guanella Pass.

Willows and tarns near Guanella Pass.

Mount Bierstadt from just below Mount Evans' summit.

HISTORY: Famed western landscape painter Albert Bierstadt was instrumental in originally naming Mount Evans "Mount Rosalie," after his future wife. In 1914, Ellsworth Bethel, the dean of Colorado mountain namers, firmly put Bierstadt's name on this summit—after it, too, had been called "Mount Rosalie" for a time.

MOUNT BIERSTADT

Low clouds and Pikes Peak from the northeast.

Pikes Peak

14,115 feet **31**

MAPS	Trails Illustrated 137–Pikes Peak/Canon City
RATING	Moderate, but long
ELEVATION GAIN	7,430 feet
ROUND-TRIP DISTANCE	24 miles
ROUND-TRIP TIME	12 to 14 hours
NEAREST TOWN	Manitou Springs
RANGER DISTRICT	US Forest Service, Pikes Peak Ranger District, 719-636-1602

COMMENT: This is a long hike with an average gradient of 11-percent. Before starting you may wish to inquire at the cog railroad about the possibility of taking the train down from the summit. Since there is a dirt road to the top of Pikes Peak, there is no register. The standard route is called the Barr Trail. You will often find RMFI and the Friends of the Peak (*www.fotp.com*) doing maintenance on the Barr Trail.

GETTING THERE: To reach the Barr Trail, drive to Manitou Springs and locate the city hall. Proceed west on US 25 (business) about 0.5 mile to Ruxton Avenue. Turn left on Ruxton Avenue and drive 0.75 mile to the Pikes Peak Cog Railroad depot, then on for a short distance to the hydroelectric plant and Hydro Street. Look for the Barr Trail parking lot and park there, if there is room.

THE ROUTE: From the south end of the parking lot, head up through switchbacks for 3 difficult miles to the top of the Manitou Incline. Ignore the mile and elevation markers, because they are wrong. Barr Camp is a relatively easy 3.5 miles from the top of the Incline. Take a break at the Barr Camp, where the trail gets steeper, moving up to an A-frame at about 12,000 feet. Follow the switchbacks to 12,800 feet, where the trail levels into a long traverse. Approximately

SIDEBAR

RACE A FOURTEENER

Every August, the Pikes Peak Marathon draws runners from around the nation. The half marathon Ascent, with 1,800 racers, is held on Saturday and the full Marathon, with 800 racers, is held on Sunday. It's mostly the same as our hiking route, with a bit added at the beginning to make the lengths 13.3 and 26.2 miles respectively. Matt Carpenter holds both records for fastest times: 2 hours and 1 minute for the Ascent and 3 hours 16 minutes for the Marathon.

1 mile from the summit you will encounter the 16 Golden Stairs that you will always remember.

Pikes Peak above timberline from Barr Trail.

HISTORY: The Arapaho name is *Heeyotoyoo'*, which means "Long Mountain" while the Utes called it *Tava*, or "Sun Mountain." Lieutenant Zebulon Pike led an expedition to the southwest part of the Louisiana Territory in 1806. In November, his team attempted to climb the "Grand Peak," but after two days without food, they turned back, citing waist deep snow and subzero temperatures. Botanist Edwin James made the first recorded ascent on July 14, 1820. After ascending the mountain by wagon and mule in 1893, Katharine Lee Bates penned the poem "America The Beautiful" that eventually became the famous song in 1910.

Pikes Peak summit view from the Pikes Peak Highway.

Pikes Peak's north face in fall.

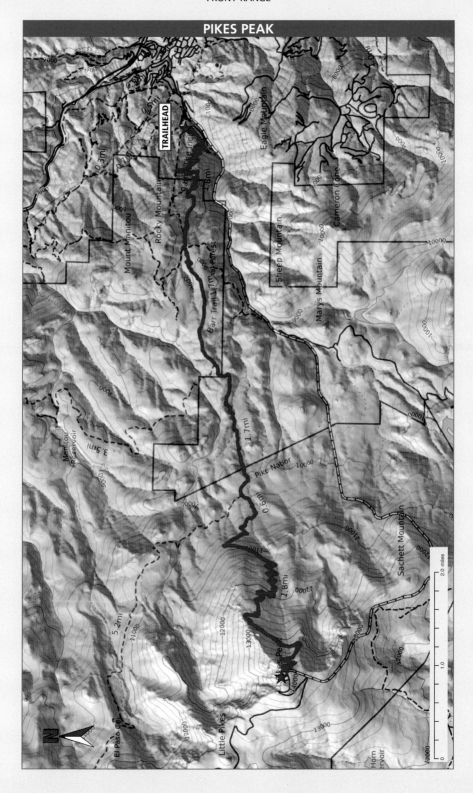

Kit Carson Peak
Challenger Point

14,165 feet 23

14,081 feet

MAPS	Trails Illustrated 138–Sangre de Cristo Mountains
RATING	Very difficult
ELEVATION GAIN	2,500 feet from Willow Lake, 6,250 feet from the trailhead
ROUND-TRIP DISTANCE	6 miles from Willow Lake, 13.5 miles from the trailhead
ROUND-TRIP TIME	8 hours from Willow Lake, 13 hours from the trailhead
NEAREST TOWN	Crestone
RANGER DISTRICT	US Forest Service, Saguache Ranger District, 719-655-2547

COMMENT: Kit Carson Avenue is memorable. The standard route follows the Willow Lake Trail and then heads up the mountain's north slope. Kit Carson Peak is on the massif Kit Carson Mountain. Challenger Point and Columbia Point are also on Kit Carson Mountain.

CFI expects to open a new trail alignment from Willow Lake to the "Rock Rib" in 2018. This map shows the new trail. Rocky Mountain Field Institute plans to have this trail completed by 2021.

GETTING THERE: Approaching from the north, go 14 miles on CO 17 from the junction of CO 17 and US 285, or, approaching from the south, go north 17 miles from Hooper on CO 17. From either direction, you next turn east on a paved road and travel 12.5 miles to Crestone. From Crestone, go east on Galena Street, reaching the trailhead after approximately 2 miles; a high-clearance vehicle is recommended beyond the forest boundary. From the Willow Creek Trailhead, hike approximately 7.5 miles to Willow Lake; campsites are available below the lake.

THE ROUTE: Take the trail around the north side of the lake and continue above the falls. It's a steep climb to Challenger Point. Over the point is the west side of Kit Carson, with a shelf called "Kit Carson Avenue." The Avenue leads around the west face of the peak and goes up the south side of the peak.

Left: Kit Carson. PHOTO BY DAVID HITE

Telephoto view of Kit Carson Mountain (left to right): Challenger Point, Kit Carson Peak, and Columbia Point.

HISTORY: Kit Carson Peak takes its name from the famous scout who, in the mid-1860s, commanded Fort Garland at the base of Blanca Peak. In 1987, the unnamed 14,081-foot northwest sub-peak of Kit Carson was named Challenger Point, commemorating the crew members of the space shuttle *Challenger*, who lost their lives on January 28th, 1986. The Latin phrase on the summit plaque translates, "To the stars through adversity." In 2003, Columbia Point (13,986 feet) on the same massif was named after the crew of the space shuttle *Columbia*, who perished on February 1st, 2003.

Kit Carson Peak from the summit of Hermit Peak, looking south

KIT CARSON PEAK | CHALLENGER POINT

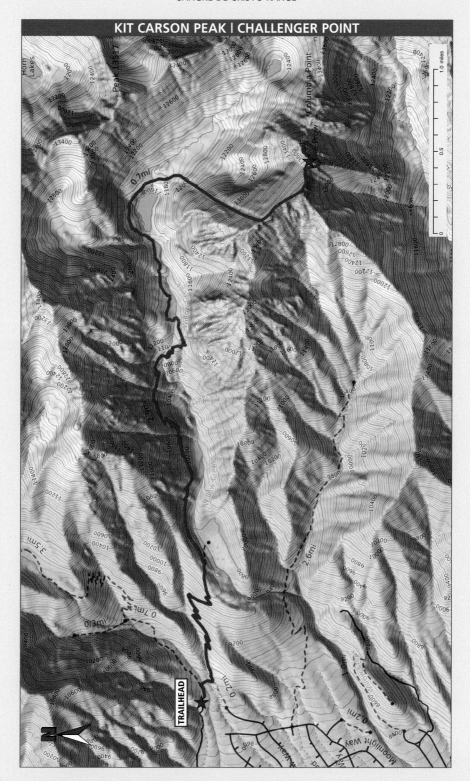

Humboldt Peak's west ridge from the North Colony–South Colony saddle.

Humboldt Peak   14,064 feet 37

MAPS	Trails Illustrated 138–Sangre de Cristo Mountains
RATING	Moderate
ELEVATION GAIN	2,400 feet from lower South Colony Lake, 4,200 feet from the trailhead
ROUND-TRIP DISTANCE	3.5 miles from lower South Colony Lake, 8.5 miles from the trailhead
ROUND-TRIP TIME	5 hours from lower South Colony Lake, 10 hours from the trailhead
NEAREST TOWN	Westcliffe
RANGER DISTRICT	US Forest Service, San Carlos Ranger District, 719-269-8500

COMMENT: Of the four mountains in the "Crestones"—Crestone Peak, Crestone Needle, Kit Carson, and Humboldt—Humboldt is the easiest. The standard route goes from South Colony Lake up to the saddle and then follows the West Ridge to the summit.

GETTING THERE: From Westcliffe, drive southeast about 4.5 miles on CO 69 toward Walsenburg. Turn right (south), go 5.5 miles to the end of Colfax Lane (CR 119), then turn right again. You are now headed straight west toward the Crestones. After about 1 mile, the road becomes very rugged, but 4WD vehicles with good ground clearance can be driven 2.5 miles up the road to a gate, where you will find a parking lot for 40 vehicles, and 10 designated camping sites. The South Colony Lakes are about 4.5 miles from the gate.

THE ROUTE: From lower South Colony Lake, hike northwest on the trail up South Colony Creek to the east side of upper South Colony Lake. Follow the Humboldt Trail north up scree and talus to Humboldt's west ridge. Reach the ridge just east of the 12,850-foot connecting saddle between Humboldt and Crestone peaks. Climb east on the ridge for less than a mile to the summit.

SIDEBAR   THE ROAD

No one is kidding about this alleged road up to the Crestone Group. Even though it gets bladed every once in a while, it is usually awful. If you do not have a 4WD vehicle with high clearance, stop at the lower trailhead. It will add 1,000 feet of elevation gain and 5 miles to the round trip. But it sure beats getting stuck!

Sunset on (left to right)
Crestone Needle (barely visible),
Mount Adams, Crestone Peak, and
Columbia/Kit Carson/Challenger,
from the summit of Hermit Peak.

Mount Bierstadt
from Guanella Pass.

HISTORY: This peak was named in honor of Alexander von Humboldt, an eminent German geographer and mountaineer who made an unsuccessful 1802 assault on Ecuador's Mount Chimborazo, then thought to be the highest peak in the world. Humboldt was officially climbed in 1883, but it is likely that miners reached the summit before that.

HUMBOLDT PEAK

TRAILHEAD

Crestone Peak   14,294 feet 7

MAPS	Trails Illustrated 138–Sangre de Cristo Mountains
RATING	Very difficult
ELEVATION GAIN	2,600 feet from lower South Colony Lake, 4,300 feet from the trailhead
ROUND-TRIP DISTANCE	4 miles from lower South Colony Lake, 13 miles from the trailhead
ROUND-TRIP TIME	8 hours from lower South Colony Lake, 12 hours from the trailhead
NEAREST TOWN	Westcliffe
RANGER DISTRICT	US Forest Service, San Carlos Ranger District, 719-269-8500

COMMENT: A climbing helmet, rope, and ice axe are highly recommended for this route. There is residual ice on the couloir near the summit well into the summer, and an ice axe may be required. Falling rock presents another hazard, making the use of a helmet a very good idea. Be careful. The standard route is from lower South Colony Lake up the South Face.

GETTING THERE: From Westcliffe, drive southeast about 4.5 miles on CO 69 toward Walsenburg. Turn right (south), go 5.5 miles to the end of Colfax Lane (CR 119), then turn right again. You are now headed straight west toward the Crestones. After about 1 mile, the road becomes very rugged, but 4WD vehicles with good ground clearance can be driven 2.5 miles up the road to a gate, where you will find a parking lot for 40 vehicles, and 10 designated camping sites. The South Colony Lakes are about 4.5 miles from the gate.

THE ROUTE: Circle lower South Colony Lake to the south and west. Climb southwest to the saddle between Crestone Needle and Broken Hand Peak. Drop down from Broken Hand Pass to the southwest and around Cottonwood Lake, moving in a westerly direction. Looking north, you will see the south face of Crestone Peak and the red couloir. The route follows the red couloir to a difficult summit.

Left: Crestone Needle (left) and Crestone Peak (right) from the Humboldt saddle.

Crestone Needle (left) and Crestone Peak (right) from the Humboldt saddle.

HISTORY: Rugged, isolated, and unforgiving, Crestone Peak dominates an area of the central Sangre de Cristo Range that until 1967 did not even have an adequate topographic map. In 1921, five years after the first ascent, the CMC named the peak. The word Crestone is from the Spanish "cresta," meaning the top of a cock's comb or the crest of a helmet.

The Crestones and Kit Carson groups.

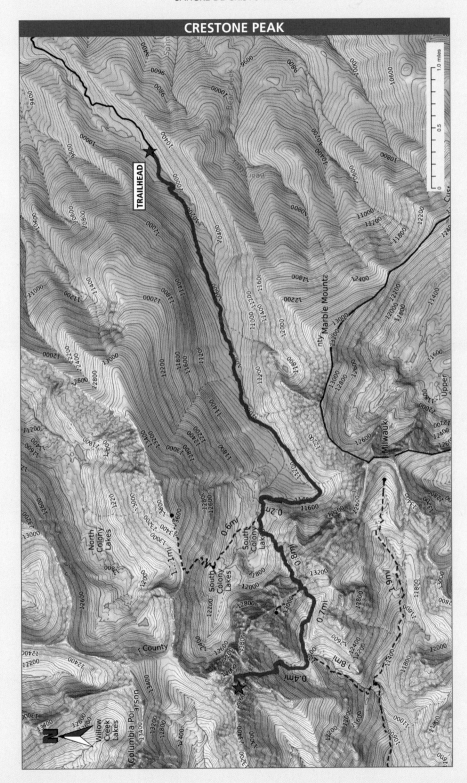

CRESTONE PEAK

Crestone Needle   14,197 feet   21

MAPS	Trails Illustrated 138–Sangre de Cristo Mountains
RATING	Very difficult
ELEVATION GAIN	2,500 feet from lower South Colony Lake, 4,200 feet from the trailhead
ROUND-TRIP DISTANCE	3 miles from lower South Colony Lake, 5.5 miles from the trailhead
ROUND-TRIP TIME	6 hours from lower South Colony Lake, 10 hours from the trailhead
NEAREST TOWN	Westcliffe
RANGER DISTRICT	US Forest Service, San Carlos Ranger District, 719-269-8500

COMMENT: This peak, once considered unclimbable, was the last of the Colorado Fourteeners to be summited. The various routes up the east face are technical climbs. Though it is a good precaution to carry a rope, the south face can, with care, be climbed unassisted. For this route, wearing a helmet is strongly recommended. The standard route is from lower South Colony Lake up the South Face.

GETTING THERE: From Westcliffe, drive southeast about 4.5 miles on CO 69 toward Walsenburg. Turn right (south), go 5.5 miles to the end of Colfax Lane (CR 119), then turn right again. You are now headed straight west toward the Crestones. After about 1 mile, the road becomes very rugged, but 4WD vehicles with good ground clearance can be driven 2.5 miles up the road to a gate, where you will find a parking lot for 40 vehicles, and 10 designated camping sites. The South Colony Lakes are about 4.5 miles from the gate.

THE ROUTE: Circle lower South Colony Lake to the south and west. Climb southwest to the saddle between Crestone Needle and Broken Hand Peak. Continue northwest along the ridge toward the Needle. About 0.2 mile above the first bench, angle slightly right and look for a cairn-marked zigzag route on grass shelves. This route leads to the third pinnacle northeast of a low point on the ridge. Drop slightly into a narrow couloir and climb abruptly up to the summit. Look for a cairned route and follow it in your descent; otherwise, you may find yourself on a cliff overhang, and will have to climb back up or use a rope.

Left: Waterfall on South Colony Creek below Crestone Needle, sunset.

Telephoto view of Crestone Needle and the start of the Needle-to-Peak connecting ridge.

HISTORY: Crestone Needle was the last Colorado Fourteener to be climbed. Albert R. Ellingwood, grand master of early Colorado climbing, and Eleanor Davis, the first woman to climb all the Fourteeners, traversed below the spindly spires of the connecting ridge from Crestone Peak to reach the top on July 24, 1916.

The turnoff from South Colony Creek to the standard route.

CRESTONE NEEDLE

Mount Lindsey 14,042 feet 43

MAPS	Trails Illustrated 138–Sangre de Cristo Mountains
RATING	More difficult
ELEVATION GAIN	3,400 feet
ROUND-TRIP DISTANCE	8 miles
ROUND-TRIP TIME	8 hours
NEAREST TOWN	Westcliffe
RANGER DISTRICT	US Forest Service, Conejos Ranger District, 719-271-8971

COMMENT: Finding your way to the trailhead is more difficult than following the climbing route. The standard climbing route goes up the Huerfano River Valley to the Northwest Ridge. If you have the time and energy after your ascent, you can also bag the Iron Nipple (13,500 feet) since it's a relatively short side trip.

GETTING THERE: Two miles north of Walsenburg, CO 69 intersects Interstate 25 at exit 52. Take CO 69 for 25 miles to Gardner. Approximately 0.2 mile west of Gardner, take the left fork onto an unmarked county road. Drive for 13 miles, passing the town of Redwing. Take the left fork onto Forest Service Road 407 in the San Isabel National Forest and continue 4 miles to a sign identifying the private property of Singing River Ranch. Ranch owners do not permit parking or camping on their property. Please close all cattle gates as you traverse the ranch. The next 7 miles to the road's end can be rough, and are best suited for a four-wheel-drive vehicle. Park at the southwest end of the State Wildlife Area.

THE ROUTE: From the end of the road, hike 1.5 miles south on an old jeep road to the end of the marsh. Turn to the southeast and climb up the drainage to a large grassy basin west of the Iron Nipple. From the grassy basin, climb southeast under a ridge to the right. Ascend a gully before climbing up to the northwest end of the summit ridge. At approximately 13,400 feet, a cleft in the ridge offers difficulty over one short, steep point. Beyond that point this route is not difficult. The summit of Mount Lindsey is private property. Please be respectful.

Left: Mount Lindsey from the west.

HISTORY: Pioneers christened this peak "Old Baldy" for its denuded, round appearance from the San Luis Valley. At the request of the CMC, the name was changed in 1953 to honor former club president Malcolm Lindsey, who was a vital force in our organization's junior activities.

Top.
Mount Lindsey, looking southwest from the Wet Mountain valley.

Left:
Mount Lindsey from the east, along US 160.

MOUNT LINDSEY

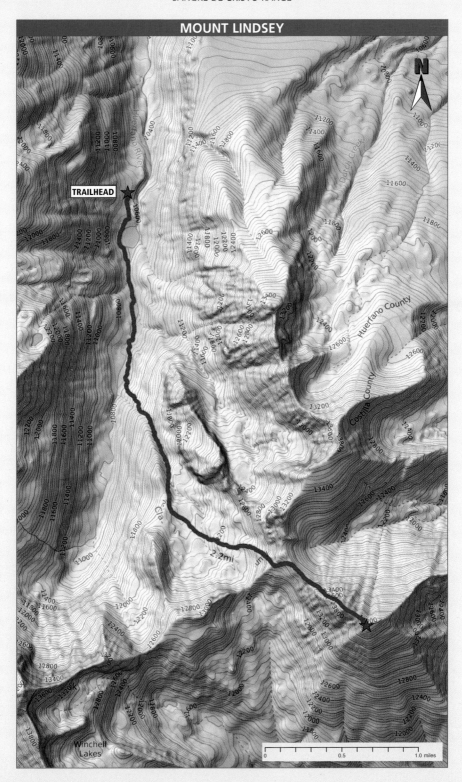

TRAILHEAD

2.2mi

Winchell
Lakes

Huerfano County

Costilla County

0   0.5   1.0 miles

Little Bear Peak   14,037 feet   44

MAPS	Trails Illustrated 138–Sangre de Cristo Mountains
RATING	Very difficult
ELEVATION GAIN	2,300 feet from Lake Como
ROUND-TRIP DISTANCE	4 miles from Lake Como
ROUND-TRIP TIME	7 hours from Lake Como
NEAREST TOWN	Blanca
RANGER DISTRICT	US Forest Service, Conejos Ranger District, 719-271-8971

COMMENT: Steep slabs and falling rock make a helmet a "must-have" on this route. The standard route is from Como Lake up the West Ridge. This is one of the most dangerous of all the Fourteeners. It is advisable to avoid crowds and make your ascent midweek.

GETTING THERE: From US 160, 6 miles west of Blanca and 15 miles east of Alamosa, drive north on CO 150 for 3 miles to a rough road going east. Take this road that becomes progressively rougher and can damage a car. We highly recommend a serious four-wheel-drive vehicle for this road. Drive as far as possible along this road, then pack in about 6 to 8 miles to Lake Como at 11,700 feet. Camp at the east end of the lake or higher, near timberline.

THE ROUTE: Continue for 0.3 mile past Lake Como on the jeep road. In the flats, head south to an obvious couloir that leads to Little Bear's west ridge. Take the ridge until it becomes steep and jagged. Turn right and contour for about 0.25 mile to a steep couloir—known as the "Hour-glass Gully" or "Bowling Alley"—that heads directly toward the summit. This is a difficult and dangerous summit. There is a route between Little Bear and Blanca that is considered to be the most difficult traverse between Fourteeners. Don't do it unless you are an experienced climber.

Left: Little Bear in winter.

Little Bear Peak from the south, with autumn cottonwoods.

HISTORY: In 1888, Charles Fay and J. R. Edmands set out to climb Blanca Peak, but ended up on what was then called West Peak. By this error, they made the first ascent of what came to be called Little Bear in 1916. Between Little Bear and Blanca lay a narrow ridge that Franklin Rhoda described as being "perfectly impassable to man."

Little Bear Peak from Ellingwood Point.   PHOTO BY BILL MIDDLEBROOK

LITTLE BEAR PEAK

Blanca Peak 14,345 feet 4
Ellingwood Point 14,042 feet 42

MAPS	Trails Illustrated 138–Sangre de Cristo Mountains
RATING	Moderate
ELEVATION GAIN	3,200 feet, plus you lose and regain 1,000 feet on the traverse
ROUND-TRIP DISTANCE	8 miles
ROUND-TRIP TIME	8 hours
NEAREST TOWN	Blanca
RANGER DISTRICT	US Forest Service, Conejos Ranger District, 719-271-8971

COMMENT: Blanca and Ellingwood are traditionally done together. Done separately, the round-trip time for each mountain is 6 hours and the distance is 6 miles. The standard route goes from Lake Como up the South Face of Ellingwood and then over to the Northwest Ridge of Blanca (or vice versa). Keep in mind that you are a looooong way from rescue help.

GETTING THERE: From US 160, 6 miles west of Blanca and 15 miles east of Alamosa, drive north on CO 150 for 3 miles to a rough road going east. Take this road that becomes progressively rougher and can damage a car. We highly recommend a serious four-wheel-drive vehicle for this road. Drive as far as possible along this road, then pack into Lake Como at 11,700 feet. Camp at the east end of the lake or higher, near timberline.

THE ROUTE: Hike northeast up the basin, passing north of Crater Lake, toward the Blanca-Ellingwood ridge. About 2 miles from the lake, turn left to reach Ellingwood or right (south) to ascend Blanca. The least technical option for climbing both peaks is to return to where the trail split. However, if you are comfortable with moderate scrambling over loose rock, you can scramble below the ridgeline on the west side following a vague line of cairns.

Left: The North Face of Blanca Peak as seen from the Huerfano River valley.

Blanca Peak.

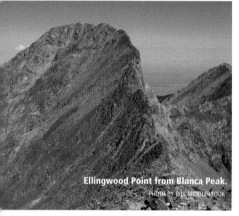

Ellingwood Point from Blanca Peak.
PHOTO BY BILL MIDDLEBROOK

HISTORY: Long a landmark, Blanca Peak has watched the march of the Ute, Spanish, and Anglo cultures across the San Luis Valley. Blanca means "white" in Spanish, and the mountain appears white most of the year—either because of snow or glistening rock. Blanca's western sub-peak is named for climber Albert Ellingwood. Considered one of the four sacred mountains by the Navajo Nation, they purchased the 16,350-acre Wolf Springs Ranch, which includes the mountain they call *Sisnaasjini* (White Shell Mountain) in 2017; the ranch will be renamed *Ma'iitsoh Bito*. In 2018, the Navajo Nation purchased the 12,500-acre Boyer Ranch, which includes Hesperus Mountain (*Dibe Ntsaa*, 13,237 feet), one of the other sacred mountains, about 140 miles away north of Durango.

The view from Crater Lake.

BLANCA PEAK | ELLINGWOOD POINT

Culebra Peak

14,047 feet **41**

MAPS	USGS Culebra Peak and El Valle Creek. There is no Trails Illustrated map for this peak.
RATING	Moderate
ELEVATION GAIN	3,000 feet
ROUND-TRIP DISTANCE	6.5 miles from the four-way intersection
ROUND-TRIP TIME	6 hours
NEAREST TOWN	San Luis
CONTACT	Cielo Vista Ranch, 719-557-9696, Email: cvrproperty@gmail.com

COMMENT: Culebra is on private land and access is restricted. To prevent overcrowding, reservations are required for each person at *Cielovista-ranchco.com/culebra-booking.* The fee is currently $150 per person. At present, the peak is currently open all year except for August through October when it closes for hunting season; June and July are your safest bets. The standard route is the northwest ridge route. You can also climb Red Mountain (13,908 feet, Colorado's 70th highest peak).

GETTING THERE: From either Alamosa drive east or from Walsenberg drive west on US 160 to Fort Garland. Go south on CO 159 to San Luis, then drive south and southeast on CO 152 to the town of Chama. Turn left on L.7 (Whiskey Pass Road) and head east for 3.7 miles. After crossing a bridge, turn right onto the dirt road marked CR 25.5. Follow this about a half-mile to a "T" junction. Turn left on to CR M.5, and drive 1 more mile to the gate for Cielo Vista Ranch where someone will let you in. Proceed 2 more miles to the ranch headquarters and check in. From there, it is to the lower parking lot (called 4-Way Junction) for 2WD vehicles or 4.4 miles to the upper parking lot for 4WD vehicles.

THE ROUTE: From either trailhead, there is no trail. Cross a stream and ascend the ridge at the low point to the east; look for a large cairn at about 13,350 feet. Follow the ridge south, then southeast. Culebra's summit becomes visible at the highest point south of the ridge. Continue south, then southeast, on the ridge. There is a small loss in elevation and some rock scrambling near the summit.

Left: Culebra's summit (left) and false summit (right).

A massive cairn on Culebra's standard route.

HISTORY: The southernmost Fourteener in Colorado, Culebra misses being the highest point in New Mexico by less than ten miles. The mountain sits on private property on the remnants of old Spanish land grants. Its name is Spanish for "snake." Spanish explorers or land grant surveyors may have made the first European ascent.

Heading toward Culebra Peak's summit.

CULEBRA PEAK

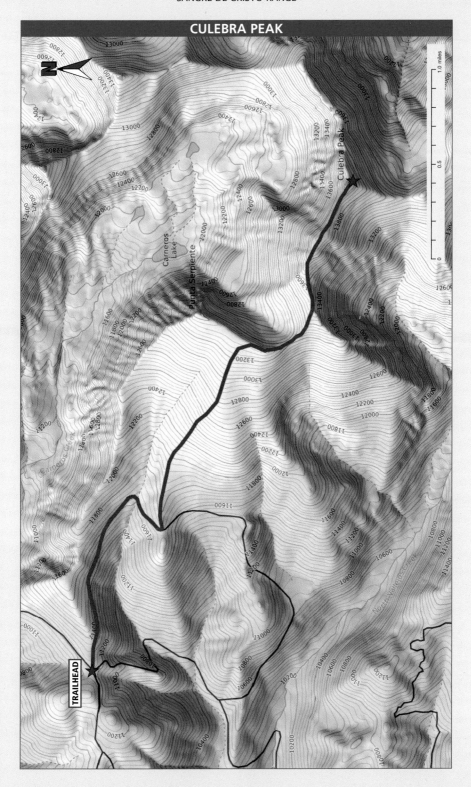

Quandary Peak   14,271 feet   13

MAPS	Trails Illustrated 109–Breckenridge/Tennessee Pass
RATING	Moderate
ELEVATION GAIN	3,300 feet
ROUND-TRIP DISTANCE	6 miles
ROUND-TRIP TIME	6 hours
NEAREST TOWN	Breckenridge
RANGER DISTRICT	US Forest Service, Dillon Ranger District, 970-468-5400

COMMENT: This is a very popular peak, particularly on weekends. The East Ridge is the standard route. While one of the easiest Fourteeners, it is also easy to lose the trail above treeline, particularly early in the season when there is still a lot of snow. The route up and down Quandary is a favorite for backcountry skiers.

CFI completed trail construction and restoration work on this peak in 2002. CFI will complete a three-year, focused trail reconstruction/ restoration effort in 2018 and maintain annually with volunteer work and their Adopt-a-Peak Program.

GETTING THERE: Drive west through the Eisenhower Tunnel on Interstate 70 and exit at Frisco, heading south on CO 9 toward Breckenridge. Continue south past the town for approximately 9 miles to where CO 9 starts to climb to Hoosier Pass. Make a right on Blue Lakes Road (CR 850). You will be heading west up a canyon. Immediately thereafter, an unimproved road angles up to the right from CR 850. Take McCullough Gulch Road (CR 851) to the trailhead and parking lot 0.1 mile from CR 850. If the parking lot is full, do not park in front of homes; either use the overflow lot just past the trailhead or return to the junction with CR 850.

THE ROUTE: The trail is across the road and leads west through timber. Near treeline, the trail follows the south side of the long east ridge of the peak. At about 12,900 feet, the trail joins the main ridge and continues over tundra and talus to the summit.

Left: Looking northwest from Beaver Ridge to Quandary Peak.

A telephoto view of Quandary Peak from the northeast.

HISTORY: Quandary Peak reportedly gets its name from miners who were in a quandary over the proper identification of a mineral specimen found on its slopes. The fact that the peak was variously referred to as McCullough's Peak, Ute Peak, and Hoosier Peak may have left just about everyone in a quandary as to its name.

Quandary's north face reflected in a beaver pond in McCullough Gulch.

SIDEBAR / CELL PHONES

Take one with you. Turn it off. Cell phones don't work in the valleys and on approaches, but they sometimes work at altitude. A cell phone is a radio. Leaving it on all the time will drain the battery. If there is an emergency, use your map or GPS (if you have one) to identify the location (longitude and latitude or UTM coordinates) of the incident and call 911. If your cell doesn't acquire a signal, keep going higher, and keep trying.

QUANDARY PEAK

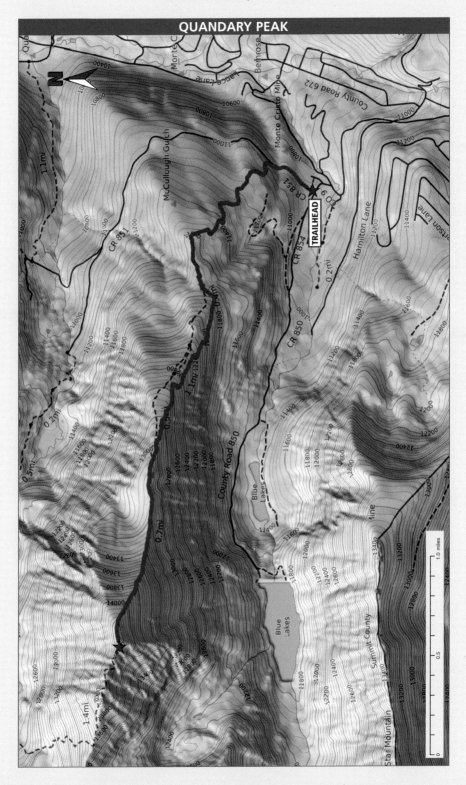

Mount Lincoln at sunrise from near the summit of Mount Bross, looking north. (Quandary rises beyond.)

Mount Democrat 14,155 feet 28
Mount Cameron 14,238 feet *
Mount Lincoln 14,293 feet 8
Mount Bross 14,172 feet 22

MAPS	Trails Illustrated 109–Breckenridge/Tennessee Pass
RATING	Moderate
ELEVATION GAIN	3,700 feet
ROUND-TRIP DISTANCE	7 miles
ROUND-TRIP TIME	8 hours
NEAREST TOWN	Alma
RANGER DISTRICT	US Forest Service, South Park Ranger District, 719-836-2031

COMMENT: The standard route is a loop that goes up to Mount Democrat, then to Mount Cameron, Mount Lincoln, and below the summit of Mount Bross before returning to Kite Lake. This circuit makes for a long day.

As of 2009, conditional access has been granted by private landowners to Mount Democrat and Mount Lincoln (as well as over the sub-peak, Cameron). The summit of Mount Bross remains closed to the public, although you can still complete the full trail loop skirting beneath the summit of Bross (CMC counts this deviation as a summit).

CFI has partnered with local landowners, CMC, Mosquito Range Heritage Initiative, and the US Forest Service to regain access to these mountains. (All of these summits were closed to public access in 2006 until early 2009.) Those of us at CFI and CMC cannot stress enough how important it is that you stay on the trail at all times, respect trail signage, stay off of closed routes, and stay away from old mines and mine structures. The 2009 reopening of access to Democrat and Lincoln is a CONDITIONAL reopening based upon your observance of the rules now, and in the future.

GETTING THERE: Drive on US 285 to Fairplay, then north on CO 9 for 6 miles to Alma. In the center of town, turn left (west) and drive 3 miles up Buckskin Creek Road (also called Secondary Forest Route 416) to Kite Lake.

THE ROUTE: From Kite Lake, follow the trail north 2 miles to the saddle. Climb Democrat 0.5 mile to the southwest. Return to the saddle and climb northeast for another 0.5 mile over Mount Cameron, and then an easy 0.5 mile to the summit of Mount Lincoln. Return to the Mount Cameron-Lincoln saddle and follow the gentle trail southeast 1 mile to Mount Bross. Return to Kite Lake for 1.5 miles down the west slope of Bross, taking the trail along the ridge. Continue down a couloir to the old road and back to the lake.

HISTORY: In 1861, Wilbur F. Stone, who later helped draft Colorado's Constitution, climbed the highest summit west of Hoosier Pass and suggested that it be named in honor of the recently elected president of the United States, Abraham Lincoln, a Republican. In protest, Southern miners renamed Buckskin Peak to Mount Democrat during the Civil War. Mount Bross was named for William Bross, a lieutenant governor of Illinois, who owned mining property near Alma.

The west slopes of Mount Bross reflect in a rocky tarn above Lake Emma

Mount Lincoln.

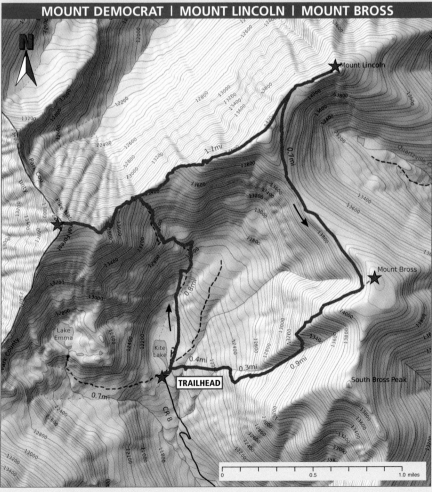

MOUNT DEMOCRAT | MOUNT LINCOLN | MOUNT BROSS

Mount Sherman 14,036 feet 45

MAPS	Trails Illustrated 110–Leadville/Fairplay
RATING	Moderate
ELEVATION GAIN	2,100 feet
ROUND-TRIP DISTANCE	5 miles
ROUND-TRIP TIME	2.5 hours
NEAREST TOWN	Fairplay
RANGER DISTRICT	US Forest Service, South Park Ranger District, 719-836-2031

COMMENT: For a more interesting trip, you can climb Mount Sheridan (13,768 feet) first, then drop to the saddle and continue up the long ridge to the summit of Mount Sherman. The standard route is the Southwest Ridge. The Day Mine Company of Leadville, which permits climbers to go through its property to the summit, owns the entire mountain.

GETTING THERE: Drive on US 285 to Fairplay, then continue south past the town for about 1 mile. Turn west (right) on Park CR 18 (also called 4 Mile Creek Road) to Fourmile Creek. Drive 10 miles to the site of Leavick, a ghost town. Continue 2 miles and park below a gate at 12,000 feet.

THE ROUTE: Begin hiking on the road and pass the first mine, the Dauntless. Hike northwest up the most obvious road to the abandoned Hilltop Mine, then follow a trail up to the saddle between Mount Sheridan and Mount Sherman. Turn north (right) and hike up the ridge about 1 mile to the summit of Mount Sherman.

SIDEBAR / SUMMIT TIME

Don't be surprised, on reaching the summit of a Fourteener, to find fifty or so other climbers sprawled all over the rocks. The very first thing you should do when you summit is look around 360 degrees for a thunderstorm. Next, check that everyone in your crowd is feeling okay, then sit down for a snack and rehydration. We have spent as little time on the summit as it takes to sign the register and beat feet downhill in front of a thunderstorm, and we have also lollygagged for an hour or so at 14,000 feet.

Left: Dauntless Mine and Mount Sherman summit.

Hilltop Mine and Mount Sherman summit.

HISTORY: Mount Sherman's namesake is probably Civil War general William Tecumseh Sherman. As in the rest of the Mosquito Range, mining activity on the mountain was frenzied, and a first ascent by miners in the 1860s is almost a certainty. In 1967, a Cessna 310 made an emergency landing on its broad summit plateau.

The west slopes of Mount Sherman, viewed from Iowa Gulch.

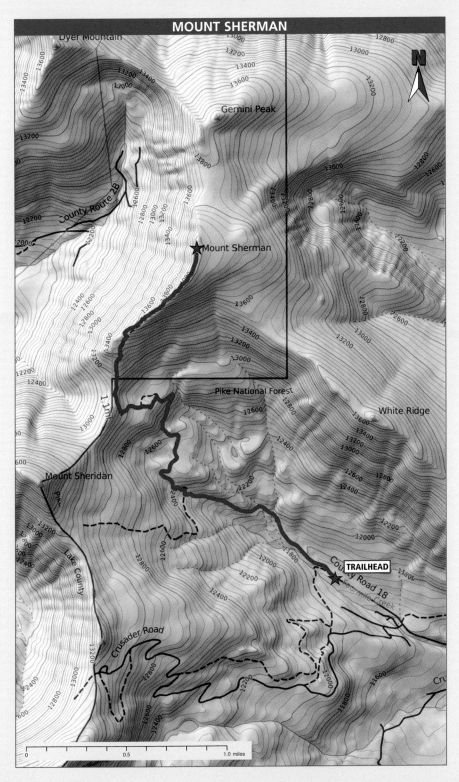

MOUNT SHERMAN

Dyer Mountain

Gemini Peak

County Route 2B

★ Mount Sherman

1.1 mi

Pike National Forest

White Ridge

Mount Sheridan

Lake County

Crusader Road

TRAILHEAD

County Road 18

0   0.5   1.0 miles

Mount of the Holy Cross.

Mount of the Holy Cross

14,009 feet

MAPS	Trails Illustrated 126–Holy Cross/Ruedi Reservoir
RATING	Moderate, but long
ELEVATION GAIN	5,600 feet
ROUND-TRIP DISTANCE	12 miles, feels like 20
ROUND-TRIP TIME	10 hours
NEAREST TOWN	Minturn
RANGER DISTRICT	US Forest Service, Holy Cross Ranger District, 970-827-5715

COMMENT: When you review this route on your map, note that this is one of those routes where you lose altitude on the approach—in this case, almost 1,000 feet—that you gain and then lose and then have to gain again. On the way back down to your car, you have to climb back up Half Moon Pass. It can make you a tad grumpy. The North Ridge is the standard route. Every year, a number of climbers get lost on this route and call for help. Take a map and compass. You have been warned.

CFI completed trail construction and restoration work on the Half-moon approach in 2014, and now maintains it annually with volunteer work and their Adopt-a-Peak Program. Due to the length of this route, some people opt to camp in the East Cross Creek valley. Please note that this is a Wilderness Area that has strict regulations about camping.

SIDEBAR   **ALTITUDE SICKNESS**

Acute Mountain Sickness (AMS) can strike just about anyone at any time, at altitude. We've had flatlander friends get sick on the ride up Interstate 70 at 8,000 feet, and we've all, at one time or another, gotten AMS at different altitudes. It is simply hard to predict who will get it, or when. Some people can go from sea level to 14,000 feet with no ill effects at all, and some highly trained individuals get sick at 10,000 feet. Even more confounding, your susceptibility can change as you age. The symptoms of AMS are headache, nausea, loss of appetite, fatigue, dizziness, and sometimes vomiting.

In extreme cases, high altitude pulmonary edema (HAPE) or cerebral edema (HACE) can manifest even in Colorado. These are life-threatening illnesses that require immediate evacuation to lower altitude. If anyone experiences uncontrollable coughing, particularly with blood, or has trouble speaking or maintaining consciousness—get them down, fast!

GETTING THERE: From Minturn, drive south on US 24 for 3 miles, then turn right (southwest) and drive on Forest Service Road 701 for 8.5 miles, passing Tigiwon Campground, to Halfmoon Campground at 10,300 feet. Camp in this area.

THE ROUTE: Hike west for 2 miles to Half Moon Pass at 11,600 feet. Descend 1.7 miles and 960 feet to East Cross Creek. Follow the trail west around a small lake 0.5 mile to the ridge and bear south up the ridge for 3 miles to the summit. Be careful on the descent not to drop left (west) into the West Cross Creek drainage. Remain on the north ridge of the mountain until the trail used during the ascent can be clearly identified descending into the trees at timberline.

HISTORY: Early reports of a mountain with a cross may have referred to seams of quartz near Fletcher Mountain. The snowy cross shape on the Mount of the Holy Cross was first officially reported in 1869, when it was seen from the summit of Grays Peak. In 1873, William Henry Jackson photographed the cross, while two other Hayden Survey members made the first ascent of the mountain.

Sunrise on the Mount of the Holy Cross.

MOUNT OF THE HOLY CROSS

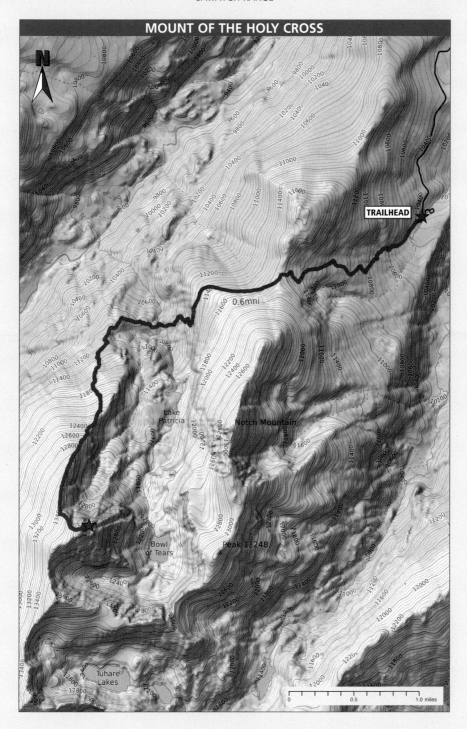

N

TRAILHEAD

0.6mni

Lake
Patricia

Notch Mountain

Bowl
of Tears

Peak 13248

Tuhare
Lakes

0   0.5   1.0 miles

Mount Massive

14,421 feet 2

MAPS	Trails Illustrated 127–Aspen/Independence Pass
RATING	Moderate
ELEVATION GAIN	4,400 feet East Trail; 3,950 feet Southwest Trail
ROUND-TRIP DISTANCE	13.5 miles East Trail; 7 miles Southwest Trail
ROUND-TRIP TIME	8 hours East Trail; 6 hours Southwest Trail
NEAREST TOWN	Leadville
RANGER DISTRICT	US Forest Service, Leadville Ranger District, 719-486-0749

COMMENT: This route along a segment of the Colorado Trail and up the east side of Massive is one of the more beautiful Fourteener trails. The standard route is up the East Slopes. However, the Southwest Slope Route is a good alternative if you don't mind a steeper climb and have a high-clearance 4WD vehicle.

CFI completed trail construction and restoration work on this route in 2009. Be sure to stay on the trail. Alpine plants take many years to reestablish—you can help by staying off of closed trails.

GETTING THERE: From Malta Junction, which is about 3 miles southwest of Leadville on US 24, drive west on CR 300 for 1 mile, then head south on FR 110 for 5.5 miles to Halfmoon Campground at 10,000 feet. Camp here, or proceed another 1.5 miles west and park at the Mount Massive parking lot, where the Colorado Trail crosses the road. You can also park at the Mount Massive overflow lot on the left. To reach the Southwest Trailhead, continue straight on CR 11 for 2.5 miles of rough dirt road.

EAST ROUTE: Take the Colorado Trail north 3 miles to the Mount Massive Trail. Follow this trail through timber, then into a bowl and onto the northeast shoulder of the summit. This trail takes you very close to the summit, but some boulder scrambling is required near the top.

SOUTHEAST ROUTE: This starts off fairly gentle as you hike along North Halfmoon Creek for 1.5 miles. Once you make the right turn towards the summit, it's a long grunt with 3,200 feet of climbing in just 2 miles.

Left: Mount Massive from the trail to Native Lake.

Looking southwest over Native Lake toward Mount Massive.

HISTORY: The Arapaho name is *Hiwoxuu hookuhu'ee*, meaning "Elk's Head," though this may apply to the entire Sawatch Range. With a broad three-mile summit crest, it has more area above 14,000 feet than any mountain the United States outside of Alaska. Henry Gannett climbed, named, and mapped the mountain for the Hayden Survey in 1873. Local sentiment in Leadville has preserved the name despite outside attempts to change it to McKinley, Gannett, or Churchill.

Moonset over a snow-covered Mount Massive.

MOUNT MASSIVE

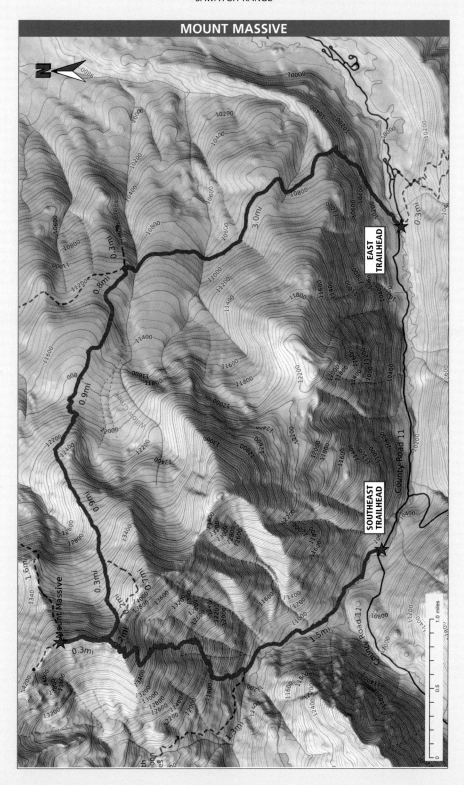

EAST TRAILHEAD

SOUTHEAST TRAILHEAD

Mount Massive

County Road 11

County Road 11

3.0mi

0.3mi

0.8mi

0.9mi

0.9mi

0.3mi

0.3mi

1.6mi

1.5mi

1.3mi

Willow Creek

N

1.0 miles

0.5

0

Mount Elbert

14,440 feet **1**

MAPS	Trails Illustrated 127–Aspen/Independence Pass
RATING	Moderate
ELEVATION GAIN	4,700 feet NE Ridge, 4,900 feet E Ridge, 4,900 feet SE Ridge
ROUND-TRIP DISTANCE	9.5 miles NE Ridge, 14 miles E Ridge, 11 miles SE Ridge
ROUND-TRIP TIME	8 hours NE Ridge, 10 hours, E Ridge, 12 hours, SE Ridge
NEAREST TOWN	Leadville
RANGER DISTRICT	US Forest Service, Leadville Ranger District, 719-486-0749

COMMENT: Mount Elbert is not a particularly striking mountain and all the routes are walk-ups, but Elbert is the highest Fourteener in Colorado and the second highest peak in the Lower 48 States. There are three standard routes: the Northeast Ridge and East Ridge are the easiest, while the Southeast Ridge is slightly more challenging. The trails on Elbert, particularly the Northeast and East Ridges, were in very bad condition.

CFI plans to complete the East Ridge Route by 2019, and restoration of the old route by 2021. Reconstruction efforts on the Northeast Ridge route are planned to begin in 2019. Reconstruction efforts on the upper slopes of the Southeast Ridge Route are slated to begin in 2023.

GETTING THERE: To get to the Northeast Ridge, from Malta Junction, which is about 3 miles southwest of Leadville on US 24, drive west on CR 300 for 1 mile, then head south on FR 110 for 5.5 miles to Halfmoon Campground at 10,000 feet. Camp here, or proceed another 1.5 miles west and park where the Colorado Trail crosses the road. There is a large parking lot on the left and a sign for the Mt. Elbert Trailhead. There are also outhouses.

To reach the East Ridge, continue south on US 24 and go west on CO 82 towards Twin Lakes. After about 4 miles, turn right on CR 24. From there, it is 1.2 miles of pavement to the lower trailhead just after the Lakeview Campground (specs above listed from here). If you have a good 4WD vehicle, continue another 50 feet and turn left on FR 125.1B and drive another 2 rugged miles to the upper trailhead (this also saves about 800 feet of elevation gain).

Left: Colorado's highest summit, viewed from the north.

For the Southeast Trail, stay on CO 82 for 10.5 miles from the turn at US 24. The trailhead is on the right.

NORTHEAST RIDGE ROUTE: This is the most popular route for peakbaggers in a hurry. Hike south on the Colorado Trail for 2 miles to a well-defined fork in the trail for the North Mount Elbert Trail. Turn right (west) and climb 3 miles up a rather steep trail (southwest) to the summit.

EAST RIDGE ROUTE: The South Mount Elbert Trail is the more relaxing way to climb the state's highest peak as it wanders through an aspen forest at the start. Much of the ascent follows the ridge but as you near the final push, the trail turns south before making the final climb to the summit. This trail is currently under construction, so the exact route may change.

SOUTHEAST RIDGE ROUTE: Arguably the most scenic and least travelled of the three routes, this follows Black Cloud Creek for about 1.5 miles and then climbs steeply to gain the ridge where the trail ends. As you follow the ridge, you cross over the South Peak of Elbert and then descend about 200 feet to the saddle before making the final climb. Note that you will be on the ridge for 2 miles each way, entirely above 13,500 feet, so keep an eye on the weather.

HISTORY: Mount Elbert is the second-highest peak in the contiguous United States, behind California's Mount Whitney (14,505 feet). It was named for Samuel Elbert, who came to Colorado in 1862 as secretary to Territorial Governor John Evans. Elbert furthered his political fortunes by marrying Evans' daughter, Josephine, in 1865. After his own tenure as territorial governor, Elbert served twenty years on the state supreme court.

Colorado's rooftop, Mount Elbert's summit.

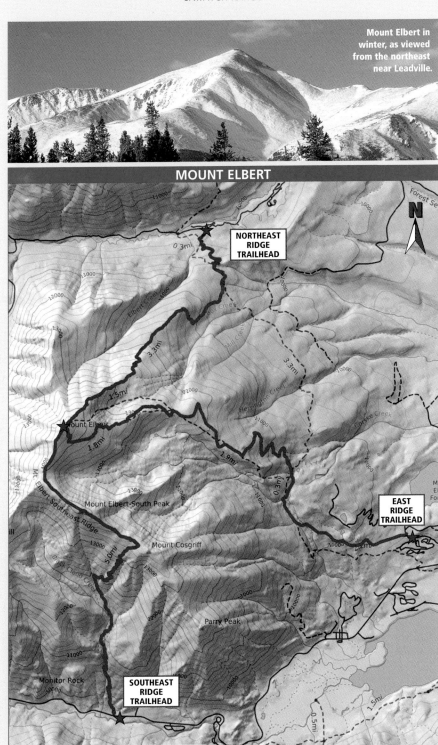

Mount Elbert in winter, as viewed from the northeast near Leadville.

MOUNT ELBERT

NORTHEAST RIDGE TRAILHEAD

0.3mi

Elbert Creek

3.3mi

3.3mi

1.5mi

Herrington Creek

Corske Creek

Mount Elbert

1.8mi

1.9mi

0.3mi

Mount Elbert-South Peak

Mount Elbert Southeast Ridge

EAST RIDGE TRAILHEAD

Mount Cosgriff

5.0mi

Parry Peak

Monitor Rock

SOUTHEAST RIDGE TRAILHEAD

1.5mi

0.5mi

0.3mi   0.9mi

0   1.0   2.0 miles

N

Forest Se

La Plata Peak

14,336 feet 5

MAPS	Trails Illustrated 127–Aspen/Independence Pass
RATING	More difficult
ELEVATION GAIN	4,500 feet
ROUND-TRIP DISTANCE	9 miles
ROUND-TRIP TIME	8 hours
NEAREST TOWN	Leadville
RANGER DISTRICT	US Forest Service, Leadville Ranger District, 719-486-0749

COMMENT: There are a number of braided trails on this route. Please stay on the designated trail marked by cairns. The Northwest Ridge is the standard route.

CFI completed construction and restoration efforts on the North-west Ridge Route in 1995, and now maintains it annually with volunteers and their Adopt-a-Peak Program. CFI does not recommend the South-west Ridge because it is an unofficial social trail that has extensive damage. There are plans for constructing a proper trail but it's low on the priority list.

GETTING THERE: From Leadville, drive toward Independence Pass on US 24, then turn west (right) onto CO 82. Continue for 14.5 miles. Look for a parking area on your left near the South Fork Lake Creek Road.

THE ROUTE: Hike along South Fork Lake Creek Road, crossing Lake Creek on a bridge, and follow signs to the trailhead. The standard route is to the west of the trail marked on the USGS quad. The first mile of the climb passes through private property. Continue through forest and meadow to the east of the ridge. Traverse south under the ridge and follow a couloir to the southeast and then up the west side of the peak. As you are approaching the ridgeline/saddle at about 12,700 feet, watch carefully for the correct trail route. Follow the rock steps and rubble walls to guide you up to this section, and do not veer right (south) into the closed restoration area. Be careful of the same on your return route. Watch along the ridgeline to the summit for occasional cairns that will keep you on-route and off of restoration areas.

Left: La Plata Peak from the east.

Sunset on La Plata Peak from Independence Pass, looking east-southeast.

HISTORY: La Plata was probably first climbed by miners in the late 1860s or early 1870s. Numerous silver mines dot its upper slopes, particularly above the mining camps of Vicksburg and Winfield. Hayden Survey members made La Plata's first recorded ascent on July 26, 1873. They gave the peak its name, which means "silver" in Spanish.

La Plata Peak, looking north from near Browns Peak's summit.

LA PLATA PEAK

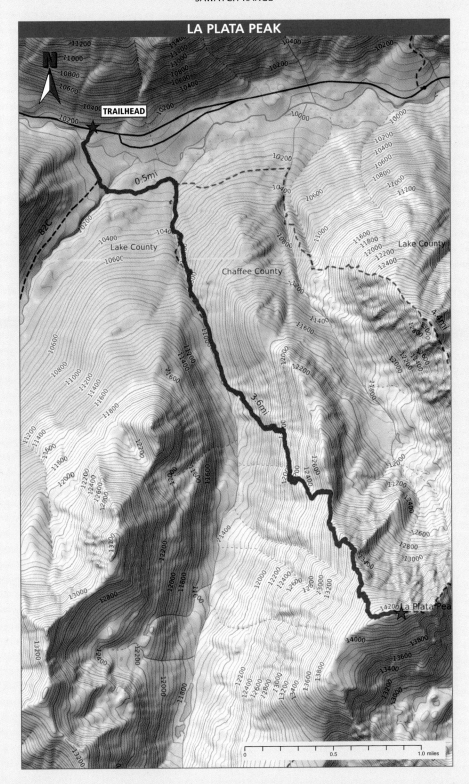

N

TRAILHEAD

0.5mi

82C

Lake County

Chaffee County

Lake County

4.4mi

3.6mi

La Plata Peak

0   0.5   1.0 miles

Mount Oxford (left) and Mount Belford (right) from the north, looking across the Clear Creek valley.

Mount Belford
Mount Oxford

14,203 feet **19**

14,160 feet **26**

MAPS	Trails Illustrated 129–Buena Vista/Collegiate Peaks
RATING	Moderate
ELEVATION GAIN	5,800 feet
ROUND-TRIP DISTANCE	11 miles
ROUND-TRIP TIME	10 hours
NEAREST TOWN	Buena Vista
RANGER DISTRICT	US Forest Service, Leadville Ranger District, 719-486-0749

COMMENT: These two peaks are traditionally climbed together. The route between Belford and Oxford entails high altitude and exposure to whatever storms are lurking as you hike about a mile in each direction. Check the weather before proceeding, since there is no shelter from sudden storms. These two peaks have a well-deserved reputation for sudden, violent electrical storms. Climb them early in the morning. The standard route is the Northwest Ridge from Missouri Gulch to Belford and then the saddle to Oxford.

CFI completed trail construction and restoration work in 1996, and now maintains it annually with volunteers and their Adopt-a-Peak Program.

GETTING THERE: From Buena Vista, drive north on US 24 for 15 miles, turn left (west) on a gravel road running along the north side of the Clear Creek Reservoir, then proceed 8 miles to the ghost town of Vicksburg at 9,700 feet. There are small and primitive camp areas along Clear Creek, east and west of Vicksburg.

THE ROUTE: Cross Clear Creek on a bridge at Vicksburg and hike south on a trail up Missouri Gulch for 2 miles, then continue along the creek until you reach timberline. You will see the route up Belford's northwest

SIDEBAR

12,000-FOOT MANTRA

After you pass 12,000 feet, the going will get tougher. It helps to repeat three or four words as a mountaineer's mantra. Here are a few of the words that will help get you up the route if mumbled over and over again between breaths: relentless, implacable, resolute, stubborn, undaunted, intrepid, headstrong, stalwart, tenacious, persistent, tireless, enduring. We have used relentless—enduring—stubborn—tenacious with some success.

shoulder. Continue on the Missouri Gulch trail to the trail junction at 11,650 feet. Take the left fork. The route climbs to the summit along a well-constructed trail. From the summit of Belford, find the trail that descends into the saddle between Belford and Oxford, dropping 700 feet. Watch the weather. Turn around if it looks at all bad. Continue east-northeast to Oxford. To descend, return to the saddle between Oxford and Belford. Return to Belford's summit via the same route. Descend using the ascent route.

Waverly Mountain (left) and Mount Oxford (right) from near Quail Mount, looking south.

HISTORY: James B. Belford was Colorado's first congressman and a powerful voice for the free coinage of silver. Belford's flaming red hair and fiery oratory earned him the nickname "the Red-Headed Rooster of the Rockies." In keeping with Collegiate Peaks' tradition, John L. Jerome Hart named Mount Oxford after the university he attended.

Mount Oxford (left) and Mount Belford (right) from the north, looking across the Clear Creek valley.

MOUNT BELFORD | MOUNT OXFORD

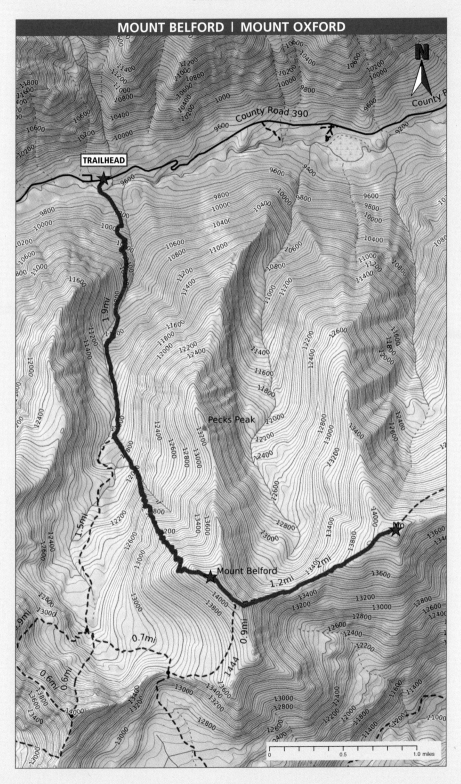

Missouri Mountain 14,074 feet 36

MAPS	Trails Illustrated 129–Buena Vista/Collegiate Peaks
RATING	More difficult
ELEVATION GAIN	4,500 feet
ROUND-TRIP DISTANCE	10.5 miles
ROUND-TRIP TIME	8 hours
NEAREST TOWN	Buena Vista
RANGER DISTRICT	US Forest Service, Leadville Ranger District, 719-486-0749

COMMENT: Be careful—Missouri Mountain can be a little more danger-ous than you would expect. The Northwest Ridge from Missouri Gulch is the standard route.

CFI completed trail construction and restoration work in 2001, and now maintains it annually with volunteers and their Adopt-a-Peak Program.

GETTING THERE: From Buena Vista, drive north on US 24 for 15 miles, turn left (west) on a gravel road running along the north side of the Clear Creek Reservoir, then proceed 8 miles to the ghost town of Vicks-burg at 9,700 feet. There are small and primitive camp areas along Clear Creek, east and west of Vicksburg.

THE ROUTE: Cross Clear Creek on the bridge at Vicksburg and hike south on the trail up Missouri Gulch for 3 miles to the head of the gulch, stay-ing to the right at the trail junction at 11,650 feet. Take the trail west up the tundra slopes and across a talus field to a saddle on the ridge. Do not take the trail that heads east toward the rocks in the vicinity of Elkhead Pass, since this is a dangerous way to the summit. Once on the ridge, proceed south, then southeast, along the narrow ridge trail to the summit. There is some exposure along the ridge trail.

Left: A tumbling creek below Missouri Mountain, looking south in Missouri Gulch.

Winter view of Missouri Mountain from high in Missouri Gulch.

HISTORY: During the silver boom of the 1880s, miners roamed the Clear Creek valley to the north of Missouri Mountain. Miners from Missouri decided to show locals their fondness for the folks back home. They named Missouri Gulch, Missouri Basin, and Missouri Mountain and probably made the mountain's first ascent.

SIDEBAR   SUN PROTECTION

Don't underestimate the intensity of UV rays at high altitudes. A bad sunburn can turn your pleasant hike into an excruciating experience. The pain from burned retinas has been described as "like pouring hot sand into my eyeballs." Apply sunscreen at the trailhead and reapply during the day. Wear sunglasses, even when it's cloudy. A good hat has a full brim to protect your ears and neck.

Telephoto view of Missouri Mountain, looking southwest from near Quail Mountain.

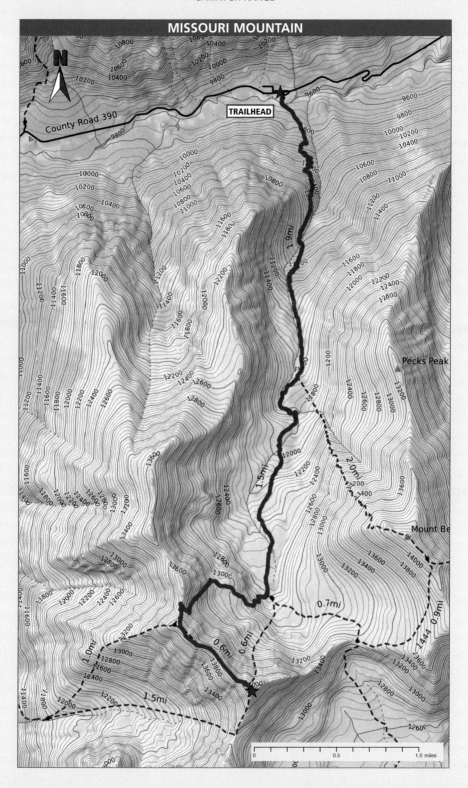

MISSOURI MOUNTAIN

TRAILHEAD

County Road 390

Pecks Peak

Mount Be

1.9mi

1.5mi

2.0mi

0.7mi

0.6mi

0.6mi

0.9mi

1.0mi

1.5mi

0   0.5   1.0 miles

Huron Peak

14,010 feet **52**

MAPS	Trails Illustrated 129–Buena Vista/Collegiate Peaks
RATING	Moderate
ELEVATION GAIN	3,200 feet
ROUND-TRIP DISTANCE	8.5 miles
ROUND-TRIP TIME	6.5 hours
NEAREST TOWN	Buena Vista
RANGER DISTRICT	US Forest Service, Leadville Ranger District, 719-486-0749

COMMENT: This will soon become the lowest Fourteener in Colorado, once Sunshine Peak is officially downsized. Despite that lowly ranking, it offers one of the best summit views in the Sawatch Range.

CFI completed trail construction and restoration work in 2001, and now maintains it annually with volunteers and their Adopt-a-Peak Program.

GETTING THERE: From Buena Vista, drive north on US 24 for 15 miles, turn left (west) on a gravel road running along the north side of the Clear Creek Reservoir, then go about 12 miles, driving through the ghost towns of Vicksburg and Winfield. Turn left at Winfield and drive just over 2 miles past Winfield on the rough South Fork Clear Creek Road to the trailhead. Leave your vehicle there.

THE ROUTE: The Huron Peak Trail is on the left of the parking lot. Follow the trail to a small creek, then cross the creek and continue up numerous switchbacks to timberline at about 11,800 feet. Stay on the trail through a large grassy basin and gain the saddle between Huron and Browns Peak, which can be seen to the north. Ascend Huron's northern rocky ridge. Stay on the ridge and follow the well-marked and cairned route to the summit. Avoid the large scree and talus bowl. Remain on the ridge for the descent and follow Huron Peak Trail back to your vehicle.

Left: Huron Peak's reflection as seen from Harrison Flat.

HISTORY: Huron Peak was likely first climbed by Ute Indians or miners. The exact origin of Huron's name is unknown, but it was probably named for a mine named Huron somewhere in the vicinity. Huron was a relative latecomer to the Fourteener ranks and was not given official US Geological Survey designation above 14,000 feet until 1956.

Above: Predawn telephoto view of Huron Peak, looking southwest from near Quail Mountain.

Right: Huron Peak, looking south from just below Browns Peak's summit.

Below: Stormy evening reflection of Huron Peak, looking northeast from Harrison Flat.

HURON PEAK

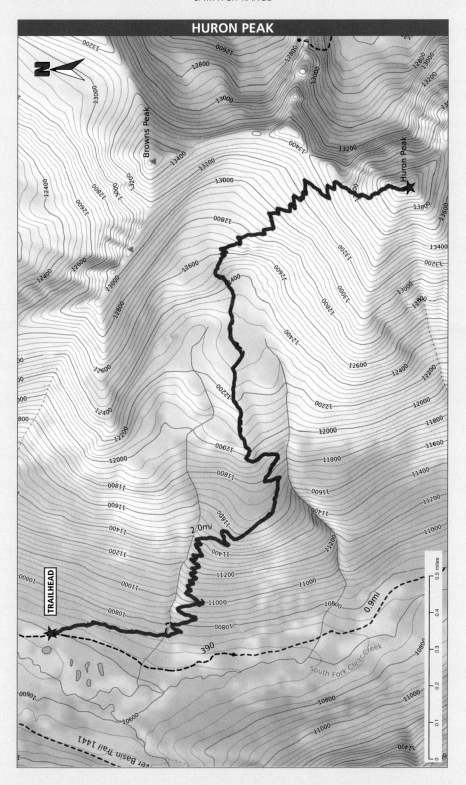

Mount Columbia.

Mount Harvard
14,421 feet 3

Mount Columbia
14,077 feet 35

MAPS	Trails Illustrated 129–Buena Vista/Collegiate Peaks
RATING	More difficult
ELEVATION GAIN	4,500 feet, plus you lose and gain 1,800 feet between Harvard and Columbia in each direction
ROUND-TRIP DISTANCE	12 miles from Horn Fork Basin camp
ROUND-TRIP TIME	12 hours from Horn Fork Basin camp
NEAREST TOWN	Buena Vista
RANGER DISTRICT	US Forest Service, Leadville Ranger District, 719-486-0749

COMMENT: It is traditional to do both Harvard and Columbia on the same day, if weather permits. The standard route is from the Horn Fork Basin up the South Slope of Harvard and then south to Columbia. Avoid the ridge between Harvard and Columbia when thunderstorms are anywhere in the area.

CFI completed trail construction and restoration work on Mount Harvard in 2002, and now maintains it annually with volunteers and their Adopt-a-Peak Program. For Mount Columbia, CFI is currently working on a multi-year trail construction and restoration project with plans to finish by 2022. Please avoid the West Slope and Southwest Couloir, either as an ascent or descent.

GETTING THERE: From Buena Vista, turn west on Chaffee CR 350 (Crossman Avenue), and drive for 2 miles, then turn north and drive for 1 mile. At the sign for North Cottonwood Creek, turn south and drive for 0.2 mile, then turn west and head west and northwest for 5 miles to the end of a passable road. Park here and backpack in.

THE ROUTE: After leaving the parking area, the trail crosses a bridge to the south side of the creek and proceeds westward 1.5 miles, to a trail junction just after the trail returns to the north side of the creek on a second bridge. Take the right-hand trail, marked Horn Fork Basin, northwest, then north 2.5 miles to timberline. Camp in this area.

From camp, follow the North Cottonwood Trail 1.25 miles to the basin below Mount Harvard. The trail veers right, up and across a talus field near Bear Lake. Continue north up the steep grass and rock ridge. Proceed under the crest of the south shoulder of the summit block, and scramble up large boulders to the summit.

The CFI-recommended non-technical route to Columbia from Harvard is to descend southeast into the Frenchman Creek drainage and then back up Columbia's north slope about a half mile from the summit. This section is 2.5 miles with 1,800 feet of elevation loss in each direction.

Return the way you came. The western scree slopes of Columbia are severely eroded and descending them could knock large rocks onto trail crews below.

HISTORY: In 1869, Josiah Dwight Whitney, a graduate of Yale and a professor at Harvard, led the first class of the Harvard Mining School into the Sawatch Range to explore rumors of 17,000-foot peaks. They climbed and named Mounts Harvard and Yale. Roger W. Toll, later superintendent of Rocky Mountain National Park, named Mount Columbia in 1916 after his own alma mater.

Mount Harvard

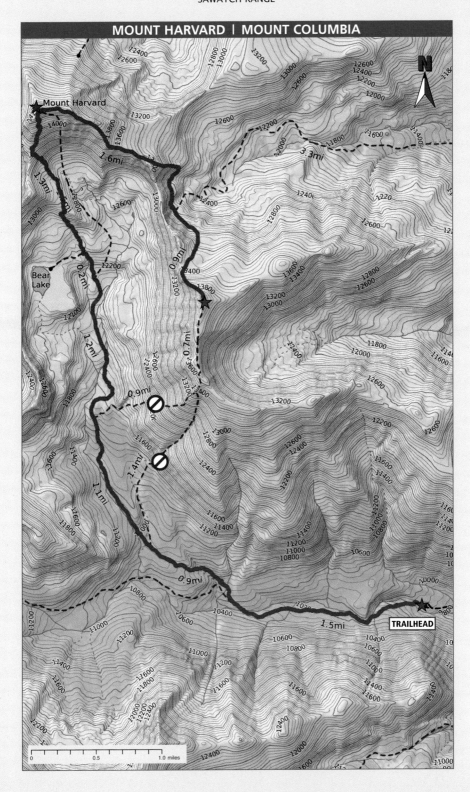

MOUNT HARVARD | MOUNT COLUMBIA

N

▲ Mount Harvard

Bear
Lake

1.6mi

1.3mi

0.2mi

1.2mi

0.9mi

0.7mi

0.9mi

1.4mi

1.1mi

0.9mi

1.5mi

TRAILHEAD

0   0.5   1.0 miles

Mount Yale

14,200 feet 20

MAPS	Trails Illustrated 129–Buena Vista/Collegiate Peaks
RATING	More difficult
ELEVATION GAIN	4,300 feet
ROUND-TRIP DISTANCE	9 miles
ROUND-TRIP TIME	8 hours
NEAREST TOWN	Buena Vista
RANGER DISTRICT	US Forest Service, Salida Ranger District, 719-539-3591

COMMENT: The original route up Mount Yale, via Denny Gulch, was so badly eroded that the Forest Service permanently closed it in 1992. The new route follows Denny Creek for the first couple miles before branching off onto the South Slope, where the trail is much more sustainable. CFI completed construction on this route in 2011.

GETTING THERE: From Buena Vista, drive west on Chaffee CR 306 along Middle Cottonwood Creek for 12 miles. Park near the Denny Creek Trailhead and sign the register (on the right side of the road).

THE ROUTE: You will be following a wide trail and will make two creek crossings. When you reach a fork, bear right and proceed northwest for 0.25 mile to an intersection that should be marked. Take the right fork into Delaney Gulch. Follow the trail to the south ridge and continue along the ridge to the summit. Descend the way you came.

HISTORY: When Yale grads climbed and named Mount Yale in 1869, they initiated the Collegiate Peaks' naming tradition. For years, Yale and Princeton alumni competed in building rock towers so their alma mater would have the honor of having the higher peak. Finally, the USGS settled the matter by officially declaring Mount Princeton as four feet taller.

Left: Mount Yale at sunset from above Cottonwood Pass.

Looking north down Ptarmigan Creek toward Mount Yale.

Cloud-to-ground lightning at 9,000 feet. You have been warned.

SIDEBAR / LIGHTNING PROTOCOL

So you are caught in the middle of a thunderstorm and lightning is striking all around you, even below. You are remembering that the temperature of lightning is somewhat in excess of the temperature of the surface of the sun, that a fairly common lightning bolt can be 500 million volts, and that lightning often travels across wet ground.

What to do? Get off the ridge. FAST. Get off the trail, because there's a good chance that it's a gully that can conduct lightning. Stay away from rock overhangs. Once you are off the ridge, put your pack and rope on the ground as an insulator. Sit on top of your pack with your arms around your knees and your feet together, close your eyes, put your hands over your ears, and think good thoughts. Try to be invisible.

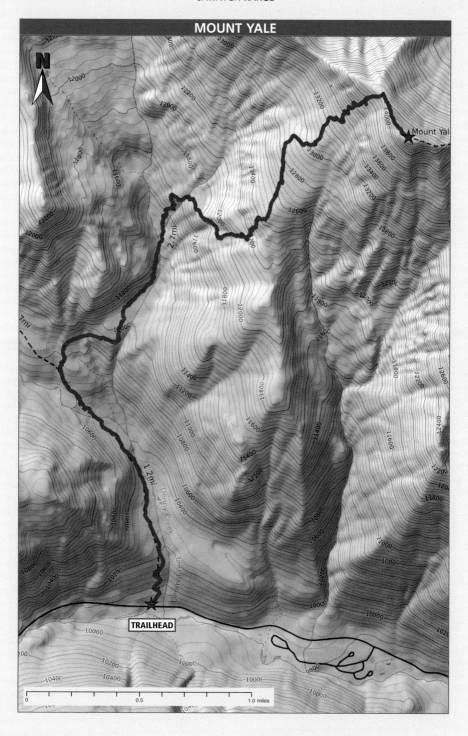

MOUNT YALE

N

Mount Yale

2.7mi

.7mi

1.2mi

Denny Creek

Denny Creek

TRAILHEAD

0   0.5   1.0 miles

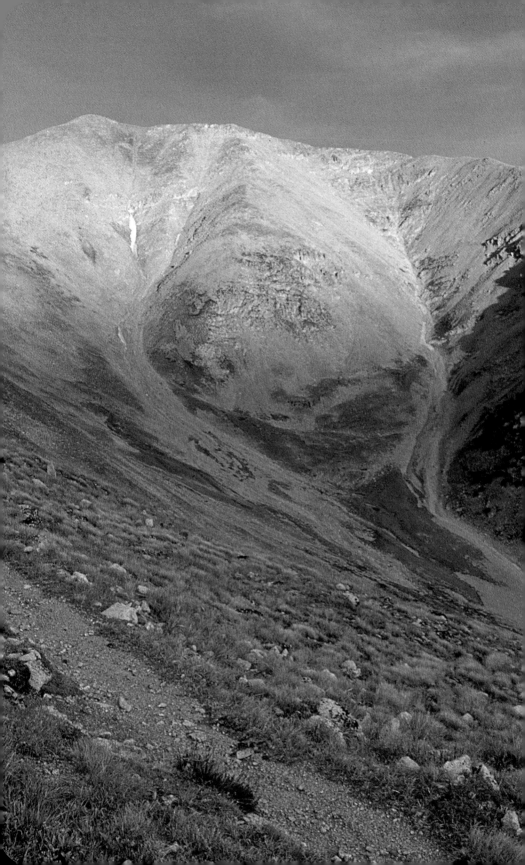

Mount Princeton

14,204 feet **18**

MAPS	Trails Illustrated 130–Salida/St. Elmo/Mount Shavano
RATING	Moderate
ELEVATION GAIN	3,200 feet
ROUND-TRIP DISTANCE	6.5 miles
ROUND-TRIP TIME	7 hours
NEAREST TOWN	Buena Vista
RANGER DISTRICT	US Forest Service, Salida Ranger District, 719-539-3591

COMMENT: On a hot summer day, you can go through a good deal of water on this route. Take extra. The standard route is from the Mount Princeton Road up the Southeast Ridge.

GETTING THERE: From Buena Vista, drive south on US 285 for 8 miles to Nathrop, then turn west on CR 162 to Chalk Creek Road. Turn right at Mount Princeton Hot Springs Inn onto CR 321. Continue 1.2 miles and turn left onto CR 322 (Princeton Road). In about a mile, there is a parking lot for 2WD vehicles at 8,900 feet. If you have 4WD with a narrow wheelbase and high clearance—and are an expert at backing up since there is no room to pass an oncoming vehicle—you can continue another 3 miles to the radio towers at 10,800 feet. There is a good campsite where the stream branches.

THE ROUTE: Hike along the road for about 1 to 1.5 miles beyond the TV relay station to where the road emerges from timber, just short of the boulder field. From this point, the A-frame Young Life chalet is visible. About 100 yards farther, a trail leaves the road uphill to the right. The trailhead is not obvious unless you go too far and look back. Follow this good trail until within 0.5 mile or less of the mine at its end. Cut left, up to a ridge that offers good access to the summit along a rocky, but usually dry, route.

Left: The trail at 12,000 feet.

Mount Princeton from the east.

HISTORY: William Libbey, Jr., a professor of geology at Princeton, made the first recorded ascent of this peak on July 17, 1877. The proximity, however, of the Hortense mine at 12,000 feet, a rich silver producer, suggests an earlier ascent by miners. The Chalk Cliffs on the mountain's south side are actually crumbling white quartz monzonite.

Mount Princeton from the northeast.

MOUNT PRINCETON

TRAILHEAD

Tigger Peak

Mount Princeton

1.9mi

Burt Gulch Road

County Road 322

Mount Antero

14,276 feet **11**

MAPS	Trails Illustrated 130–Salida/St. Elmo/Mount Shavano
RATING	Moderate
ELEVATION GAIN	3,300 feet
ROUND-TRIP DISTANCE	8 miles
ROUND-TRIP TIME	8 hours
NEAREST TOWN	Buena Vista
RANGER DISTRICT	US Forest Service, Salida Ranger District, 719-539-3591

COMMENT: Quartz, aquamarine, and topaz crystals are common in this area, and you may come across geologists and miners who have driven up to near the summit on the jeep road. This is not exactly your "one-with-the-mountain" climbing experience. It is more of a "four-wheel-drives-careening-downhill-get-the-right-of-way" sort of experience. The standard route starts in Baldwin Gulch and goes up the West Slope.

GETTING THERE: From Buena Vista, drive south on US 285 for 8 miles, then turn west on CR 162 for 9.5 miles to Cascade Campground. Camp here, and in the morning, drive another 2 miles west on CR 162 to Baldwin Gulch Road at 9,240 feet. Turn left (south) and follow the rugged road (CR 277) for 3 miles to a creek crossing at about 11,000 feet and park. This road is for 4WD vehicles; how high you can drive depends on your skills, the ruggedness of your vehicle, and snow conditions.

THE ROUTE: Hike across the creek and follow the road, which has a number of switchbacks up the broad slopes above you. Stay on the road until just short of the summit. The final ascent is up a trail through talus.

The CFI strongly requests that you follow the switchbacks. Inconsiderate hikers have created a more direct social trail that has serious erosion problems. There is a plan to address the problem but, in the meantime, please don't make matters worse due to laziness.

Left: Looking north to Mount Antero from Mount White.

Looking northwest to Mount Antero from Mount White.

HISTORY: Antero was a prominent Ute chief who promoted peace with the incoming white settlers. Nathaniel Wanemaker discovered Mount Antero's famous blue aquamarine crystals in 1884. In recent years, good gem finds have decreased, but Mount Antero remains the highest mineral locality in North America.

Mount Antero from the northeast.

MOUNT ANTERO

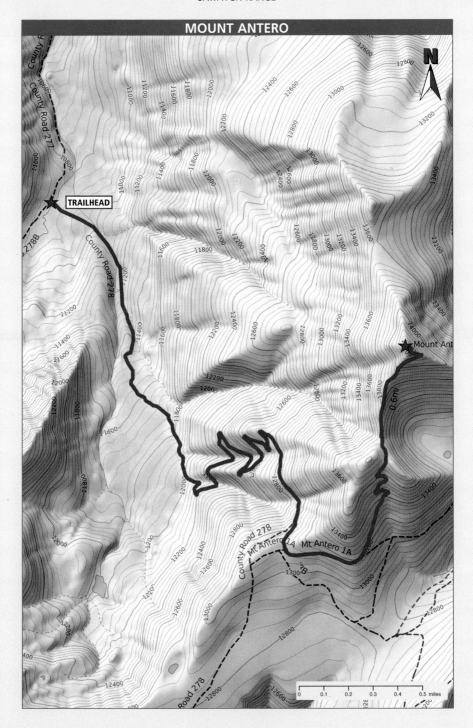

Tabeguache Peak.

Mount Shavano
Tabeguache Peak

14,231 feet 17

14,162 feet 25

MAPS	Trails Illustrated 130–Salida/St. Elmo/Mount Shavano
RATING	Moderate
ELEVATION GAIN	5,450 feet
ROUND-TRIP DISTANCE	10.5 miles
ROUND-TRIP TIME	9 to 10 hours
NEAREST TOWN	Poncha Springs
RANGER DISTRICT	US Forest Service, Salida Ranger District, 719-539-3591

COMMENT: These two Fourteeners are usually climbed together. The US Forest Service and the Colorado Fourteeners Initiative recommend that Shavano be climbed first and Tabeguache (pronounced TAB-uh-wahch) be climbed second. Starting in Blank Gulch and ascending the East Slope of Shavano, then traversing the ridge, is the standard route.

The CFI strongly recommends against using the Jennings Creek approach to the West Ridge of Tabeguache, as it is seriously eroded and dangerous with very unstable soils. Hikers who use this route are undoing restoration work that has been done by CFI staff and volunteers. In addition, many people have tried to descend McCoy Gulch, which guarantees they get cliffed out and spend a miserable night waiting for rescue.

In 2017, CFI purchased three mining claims, totaling 30 acres, which includes the summit of Mount Shavano. CFI plans to begin trail construction and restoration efforts in 2021 and will donate the summit lands to the Forest Service once the project is completed.

GETTING THERE: Drive on US 50 west from Salida to Poncha Springs. Go through Poncha Springs and continue west on US 50 for an additional 2 miles to CR 250. Turn north and follow CR 250 for 4.8 miles, then bear left onto CR 252 and continue for approximately another 3 miles to Mount Shavano/Tabeguache Peak Trailhead. The trailhead is at a stone monument that marks the old Blank Cabin. The monument honors L. Dale Hibbs, who promoted Rocky Mountain goat protection.

THE ROUTE: Walk northwest approximately 0.1 mile to an intersection with the Colorado Trail, then turn right and walk for 0.3 mile to the intersection with the Mount Shavano Trail. Turn west (left). From the

The Angel of Shavano from the east.

HISTORY: Mount Shavano, Tabeguache Peak, neighboring Mount Antero, and Uncompahgre Peak are the only four Fourteeners that bear names of Native American origin. Shavano was a prominent chief of the Tabeguache band of Utes. His name appears on the mountain on maps as early as 1875.

Colorado Trail intersection to the saddle just south of Mount Shavano is 3.5 miles. From this point on, the trail is not clearly marked. Follow the ridge to the summit of Mount Shavano, approximately 0.5 mile ahead of you. From the summit of Shavano, descend northwest for 0.75 mile to the saddle at 13,700 feet, then climb 0.25 mile west to Tabeguache's summit. Return by the same route. Do not try to skirt Shavano's summit on the way back, since you may end up in McCoy Gulch and in trouble.

Tabeguache Peak (left) and Mount Shavano (right) from the south.

MOUNT SHAVANO | TABEGUACHE PEAK

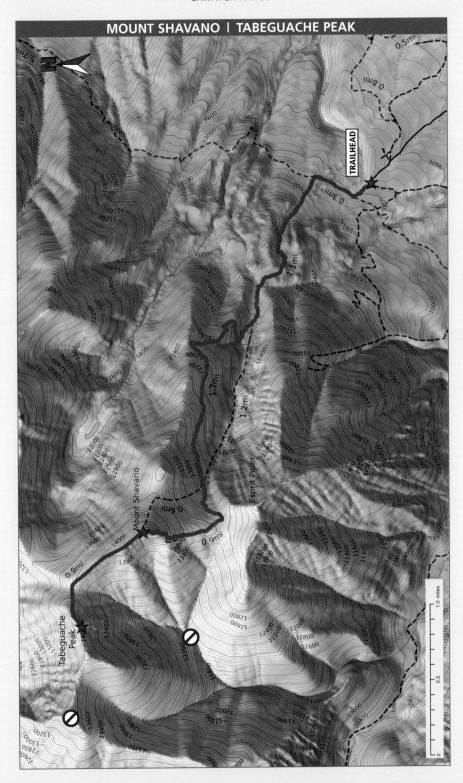

Capitol Peak is both beautiful and deadly.

Capitol Peak

14,130 feet 30

MAPS	Trails Illustrated 128–Maroon Bells/Redstone/Marble
RATING	Very difficult
ELEVATION GAIN	5,300 feet
ROUND-TRIP DISTANCE	17 miles
ROUND-TRIP TIME	16 hours
NEAREST TOWN	Aspen
RANGER DISTRICT	US Forest Service, Aspen Ranger District, 970-925-3445

COMMENT: This is the most technically difficult of the standard routes on Colorado's Fourteeners and features the infamous Knife Edge. Do not, repeat DO NOT, attempt to shortcut to Capitol Lake on your descent—there is no safe way down! Watch the weather constantly. The ridge is exposed, and lightning storms are frequent from April to September. The standard route starts at Capitol Lake and goes up the Northeast Ridge.

GETTING THERE: From Aspen, drive approximately 14 miles toward Glenwood Springs on CO 82 until you reach CR 11 on the left. Turn left (south) and drive almost 2 miles. Keep right at the fork and continue less than 0.5 mile to the next fork. There, keep left. Continue 1.5 miles southwest to another fork. Take the right fork. Follow CR 9 for approximately 4 miles, to an area where there are several cabins to the right of the road. Most passenger cars should be able to drive another 1.5 miles to a meadow at 9,400 feet.

THE ROUTE: The Capitol Creek Trail drops 400 feet to the left of the meadow, but a jeep road leaves the upper end of the meadow to Williams Lake and Hardscrabble Lake. At the point where the jeep road crosses a ditch on a bridge, there is a trail that follows the ditch to the left of the road. This trail joins the Capitol Creek Trail without the 400-foot loss in elevation, but you may encounter a problematic stream crossing, especially during runoff, before you can rejoin the trail.

Backpack south from the meadow for 6.5 miles along Capitol Creek Trail to the north end of Capitol Lake at 11,600 feet. Camp here. Follow all the Forest Service regulations when you camp, since camping rules are enforced vigorously in this area.

From the lake, the Capitol Creek Trail climbs east 0.5 mile to the Capitol-Daly ridge. Traverse several hundred feet on the east side of the ridge, then turn right and ascend to K2. Climb around the north side of K2 to reach the ridge before the Knife Edge. This 100-foot crux offers extreme exposure but just requires extreme care. After crossing the Knife Edge, do an ascending traverse following cairns, to gain the northwest ridge. Follow the ridge to the summit.

Return the way you came. Did we mention do not attempt a short cut to Capitol Lake? Don't do it. It may appear tantalizingly close but all possible routes cliff out. You. Will. Die.

HISTORY: Capitol Peak was named by the Hayden Survey for its resemblance to the US Capitol. Survey members made no attempt to climb it, because "its prism-shaped top and precipitous sides forbid access." This assessment held true until Percy Hagerman and Harold Clark reached the summit on August 22, 1909, via the knife-edged northeast ridge.

Capitol Peak from Silver Creek Pass.

CAPITOL PEAK

TRAILHEAD

2.4mi

1.2mi

0.9mi

1.3mi

0.3mi

0.7mi

0.7mi

2.8mi

1.6mi

1.2mi

4.3mi

3.3mi

2.2mi

2.7mi

3.1mi

Capitol Creek

0.4mi

2.6mi

K2

Capitol Peak

Clark Peak

Copper Creek

Pierre Lakes

Pierre Lakes

9000

10000

10000

10000

9000

9000

9000

10000

11000

10000

11000

12000

11000

10000

11000

12000

12000

12000

12000

12000

12000

12000

11000

12000

13000

13000

10000

11000

10000

0   1.0   2.0 miles

Snowmass Mountain from Lead King Basin.

Snowmass Mountain 32

14,099 feet

MAPS	Trails Illustrated 128–Maroon Bells/Redstone/Marble
RATING	More difficult or very difficult, depending on route
ELEVATION GAIN	5,800 feet from trailhead; 3,100 feet from Snowmass Lake
ROUND-TRIP DISTANCE	22 miles from trailhead; 5 miles from Snowmass Lake
ROUND-TRIP TIME	18 hours from trailhead; 6 hours from Snowmass Lake
NEAREST TOWN	Aspen
RANGER DISTRICT	US Forest Service, Aspen Ranger District, 970-925-3445

COMMENT: One of the most remote Fourteeners, this also has one of the largest snowfields in the state. The standard route goes from Snowmass Lake up the Southeast Ridge. An ice axe is recommended and, depending on the time of year and line of ascent, possibly crampons as well.

CFI plans to begin construction and restoration efforts on this peak in 2023.

GETTING THERE: From Glenwood Springs, drive approximately 27 miles toward Aspen on CO 82 until you reach CR 11. Turn left (south) onto Snowmass Creek Road. After almost 2 miles, at a "T" junction, keep left and continue about 11 miles along Snowmass Creek Road to Snowmass Falls Ranch.

THE ROUTE: Backpack south 8.5 miles, gaining 2,600 feet in elevation, up Snowmass Creek to Snowmass Lake at 11,000 feet. Camp on the east side of the lake. From this approach the whole of Snowmass Mountain is in view to the right of Hagerman Peak. Hike 0.2 mile around the south shore of the lake and climb west into the basin, keeping to the right (north) of Hagerman Peak. Then, climb the snowfield onto the ridge between Hagerman and Snowmass and follow the southeast ridge to the summit. This is a moderate, but long, ascent.

The trail from Snowmass Lake to the plateau is indistinct and in terrible condition. The CFI plans to start work on this section in 2019. In the meantime, try to stay on the main trail and avoid creating new ones. When traveling off-trail, make sure to walk on durable surfaces like rock or snow. The tundra vegetation is extremely fragile and takes years to grow back.

Snowmass Mountain from the west.

HISTORY: The inspiration for naming Snowmass is easy to understand when one surveys the perennial expanse of snow in the mountain's eastern cirque. Hayden Survey members made the first ascent in 1873 and resisted suggestions to call it "Whitehouse" to complement Capitol Peak. Bill Forest and Glen Denny first traversed the jagged, four-mile-long ridge between Snowmass and Capitol in 1966.

Snowmass Mountain and Geneva Lake, looking north.

SNOWMASS MOUNTAIN

N

TRAILHEAD

0.7mi

3.3mi

2.2mi

2.7mi

0.4mi

Maroon Snowmass

East Maroon

6.4mi

Copper Creek

Bear Creek

K2

Clark Peak

itol Peak

Pierre Lakes

Pierre Lakes

Willough

East Maroon 1993

Snowmass Mountain

5mi

4.1mi

Hagerman Peak

Snowmass Peak

0   1.0   2.0 miles

Maroon Peak

14,163 feet 24

MAPS	Trails Illustrated 128–Maroon Bells/Redstone/Marble
RATING	Very difficult
ELEVATION GAIN	4,600 feet
ROUND-TRIP DISTANCE	11 miles
ROUND-TRIP TIME	12 hours
NEAREST TOWN	Aspen
RANGER DISTRICT	US Forest Service, Aspen Ranger District, 970-925-3445

COMMENT: The Maroon Bells and Pyramid Peak, which are among Colorado's most picturesque mountains, are also among the most dangerous. The primary hazards of loose and falling rock can be somewhat minimized by climbing in small parties and by going during the week, not on weekends. Wear a helmet. The standard route is from the Maroon Lake Trailhead and ascends the South Ridge. This will be a real test of your route-finding skills. Do not attempt "The Deadly Bells" unless you are fit and have a good weather window…you really, really do not want to get caught up there in a hail or snowstorm!

CFI completed trail construction and restoration work on this peak in 2013.

GETTING THERE: From Aspen, drive northwest 1.2 miles on CO 82 and turn left (south). Keep right at the fork that appears immediately on the road to Maroon Lake. Drive about 9 miles to the end of the road where there is a new designated parking lot for climbers. During the summer months, access to Maroon Lake has been restricted to buses from the parking lot.

THE ROUTE: From the north side of Maroon Lake, hike southwest to Crater Lake. Go around the western side of Crater Lake and head south for approximately 2 miles to the South Ridge, which heads west to the ridgeline and then north to the summit. Much of the route is marked with cairns, but there are also a number of cairns that mislead climbers. If you feel you are off-route, backtrack.

Left: Maroon Peak viewed from Frigid Air Pass.

Maroon Bell.

HISTORY: After their first ascent in 1908 by Percy Hagerman and Harold Clark, the Maroon Bells became a favorite destination for Colorado Mountain Club parties. On the 1940 Labor Day outing, the club had seventy-three people in base camp and forty people in the climbing party. Rock!

Telephoto view of Maroon Peak from Paradise Divide, looking northeast.

MAROON PEAK

TRAILHEAD

Maroon Lake

Crater Lake

Thunder Peak

Maroon Peak

Peak 13039

Pitkin County

1.0 miles

North Maroon Peak is a worthy
mountain for all mountaineers.

North Maroon Peak

14,019 feet

MAPS	Trails Illustrated 128–Maroon Bells/Redstone/Marble
RATING	Very difficult
ELEVATION GAIN	4,400 feet
ROUND-TRIP DISTANCE	9 miles
ROUND-TRIP TIME	10 hours
NEAREST TOWN	Aspen
RANGER DISTRICT	US Forest Service, Aspen Ranger District, 970-925-3445

COMMENT: Technically, North Maroon does not meet the definition of a "true" Fourteener because the saddle between it and Maroon Peak isn't deep enough. The maximum drop between the twin summits is 234 feet across a distance of 2,100 feet, however this traverse requires 5th class climbing over treacherous loose rock. The standard route for North Maroon is up the Northeast Ridge. Wear a helmet.

CFI completed trail construction and restoration work on this peak in 2012.

GETTING THERE: From Aspen, drive northwest 1.2 miles on CO 82 and turn left (south). Keep right at the fork that appears immediately on the road to Maroon Lake. Drive about 9 miles to the end of the road where there is a new designated parking lot for climbers. During the summer months, access to Maroon Lake has been restricted to buses from the parking lot.

THE ROUTE: From Maroon Lake, go 1.5 miles to a right fork that heads toward Buckskin Pass. Near timberline, drop west across a stream and go southwest 0.75 mile to a timberline bench. Head southeast to a rock glacier under the north face of North Maroon. Contour south around the East Ridge into a wide couloir with rocky benches. Climb this couloir for about 0.3 mile to 12,600 feet. Exit the couloir on the left and turn a corner to ascend a second couloir. Eventually this couloir runs into the summit ridge at 13,200 feet. Cross through cliffs to reach the ridge crest and the north face. Proceed west to a chimney that can be climbed with a basic amount of technical knowledge. Climb west along the ridge to the summit.

North Maroon Peak dominates the view from Crater Lake. Maroon Peak rises behind.

HISTORY: The Hayden and Wheeler surveys mapped and admired the Maroon Bells, which are named for their color and shape, but did not reach their summits. The Hayden team named the formation Maroon Mountain and regarded North Maroon as merely a sub-peak.

SIDEBAR   **TO POLE OR NOT TO POLE**

Whether or not to use trekking poles is a personal decision. On the plus side, they can reduce wear and tear on your knees, particularly on long descents, and they give your upper body a workout. The downside is the carbide tips can do quite a bit of trail damage (consider using rubber tip guards) and the noise can be irritating.

Maroon and North Maroon peaks with autumn aspens.

NORTH MAROON PEAK

Pyramid Peak   14,025 feet 47

MAPS	Trails Illustrated 128–Maroon Bells/Redstone/Marble
RATING	Very difficult
ELEVATION GAIN	4,500 feet
ROUND-TRIP DISTANCE	8 miles
ROUND-TRIP TIME	10 hours
NEAREST TOWN	Aspen
RANGER DISTRICT	US Forest Service, Aspen Ranger District, 970-925-3445

COMMENT: See the comment for Maroon Peak; the rock here is equally as bad. The Northeast Ridge is the standard route.

CFI completed trail construction and restoration work leading from the valley to the base of the amphitheater in 2004. A note about trails: When Fourteener trails are rerouted and constructed, it is primarily done to prevent and mitigate negative impacts to natural resources, particularly sensitive high-alpine vegetation. In locations like Pyramid Peak, when a trail reaches bedrock or boulders, trail construction stops, as there is no longer vegetation to be impacted. In these areas, you are responsible for route finding.

GETTING THERE: From Aspen, drive northwest 1.2 miles on CO 82 and turn left (south). Keep right at the fork that appears immediately on the road to Maroon Lake. Drive about 9 miles to the end of the road where there is a new designated parking lot for climbers. During the summer months, access to Maroon Lake has been restricted to buses from the parking lot.

THE ROUTE: Take the trail past Maroon Lake toward Crater Lake. After about 1 mile, you will reach a rocky area marked with a large cairn to the left. Take the trail southeast across a moraine and climb steeply up the trail to the amphitheater. The Northeast Ridge Route climbs directly out of the basin to the lowest saddle on the east skyline. Then keep on the southeast side of the ridge and follow it to the summit.

Left: Pyramid Peak.

Left: Pyramid Peak
from the trail to
Buckskin Pass.

HISTORY: Originally called "Black Pyramid" by the 1874 Hayden Survey, the first documented ascent came when Percy Hagerman and Harold Clark reached the summit in August 1909. Hagerman had mining interests and Clark was a prominent Aspen attorney. Beginning in 1908, they climbed almost every major summit in the Elks.

Looking south toward Pyramid Peak from the Maroon Lake road.

Pyramid Peak from the trail to Buckskin Pass.

PYRAMID PEAK

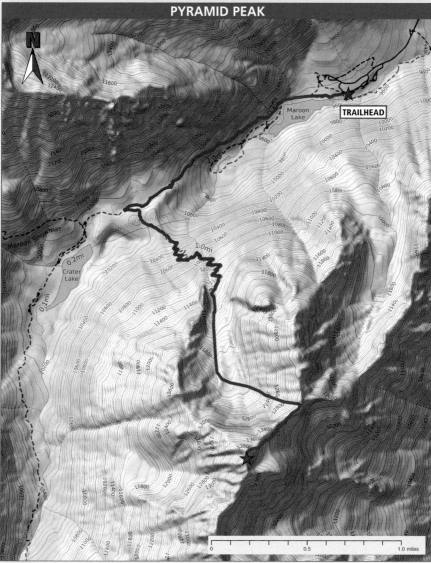

N

Maroon Lake

TRAILHEAD

Maroon Snowmas

West Maroon Creek

Crater Lake

0.2mi

0.1mi

1.0mi

1.0mi

0   0.5   1.0 miles

Castle Peak.

Castle Peak
Conundrum Peak

14,279 feet   9

14,160 feet   *

MAPS	Trails Illustrated 127–Aspen/Independence Pass
RATING	More difficult
ELEVATION GAIN	4,400 feet from the trailhead
ROUND-TRIP DISTANCE	13 miles from the trailhead
ROUND-TRIP TIME	12 hours from the trailhead
NEAREST TOWN	Aspen
RANGER DISTRICT	US Forest Service, Aspen Ranger District, 970-925-3445

COMMENT: Castle Peak is the highest, but also the least difficult to climb, in the Elk Range. Going up the Montezuma Basin to the Northeast Ridge is the standard route. Assuming the weather is good, those who are chasing the unofficial 58 Fourteeners list can traverse about a half mile northwest to Conundrum Peak.

CFI plans to start the reconstruction and restoration effort on Castle Peak in 2020.

GETTING THERE: From Aspen, drive northwest 1 mile on CO 82, then turn left (south) and take an immediate left-hand road to Ashcroft for 12 miles. Continue for 2 miles beyond Ashcroft. Turn right onto the smaller Pearl Pass Road, as the main road continues straight ahead and crosses Castle Creek. After another 0.5 mile, the road starts to climb at 9,900 feet. If using a conventional vehicle, park and camp in the aspen groves.

THE ROUTE: Either hike or use a 4WD vehicle to ascend about 2.5 miles to 11,000 feet, to the Pearl Pass Road junction, which is unmarked. Turn right and follow Montezuma Mine Road to the end, which is well over 12,000 feet. With a 4WD, this can be a very short route indeed.

One route is to climb from the end of the Montezuma Mine Road by heading southwest up the valley. At 13,400 feet, head south to gain the northeast ridge of Castle Peak. Follow the ridge to the summit. Descend by the same route, or descend the northwest ridge to the saddle between Castle Peak and Conundrum Peak. If snow is abundant and you have an ice axe, a long, exhilarating glissade is possible from the Conundrum saddle. When there is little snow, it is best to retrace your ascent route.

Castle Peak from the
Conundrum-Castle saddle.
PHOTO BY BILL MIDDLEBROOK

HISTORY: It is doubtful that Castle was climbed before 1873, when Henry Gannett led a Hayden Survey party up the difficult spires and pinnacles of its jagged south ridge. Gannett gave Castle Peak its descriptive name and reported that Castle "afforded more of a climb than any other Colorado mountain with which I have any acquaintance."

Castle Peak and Castle Lake.

CASTLE PEAK | CONUNDRUM PEAK

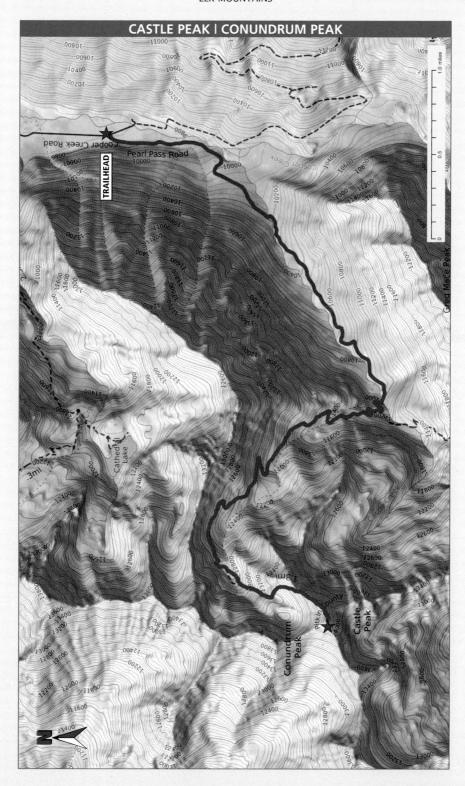

San Luis Peak from the west

San Luis Peak   14,014 feet 51

MAPS	Trails Illustrated 139–La Garita/Cochetopa Hills
RATING	Moderate
ELEVATION GAIN	3,600 feet from Stewart Creek, 3.700 feet from Willow Creek
ROUND-TRIP DISTANCE	14 miles from Stewart Creek; 11 miles from Willow Creek
ROUND-TRIP TIME	7 hours from Stewart Creek; 7 hours from Willow Creek
NEAREST TOWN	Gunnison
RANGER DISTRICT	US Forest Service, Gunnison Ranger District, 970-641-0471

COMMENT: There are two CFI routes for San Luis Peak: the Northeast Ridge and the South Ridge. While the former is better known, the biggest challenge is locating the Stewart Creek Trailhead. CFI completed both trails in 2013.

GETTING THERE: Coming from the north, take US 50 to the junction of CO 114 just east of Gunnison. It is approximately 47 miles to the trailhead from this intersection. Head south on CO 114. Drive about 20 miles and turn right onto the NN-14 road. Drive 6.7 miles to Dome Lakes and turn right onto the 15-GG dirt road (also known as FR 794 when you reach the National Forest). The road briefly goes around the lake where there is a small junction. Stay left on the main road. From the start of the 15-GG road, drive 15.7 miles to an intersection where there are signs. Follow the sign for the Stewart Creek Trailhead by continuing straight on the 794 road. Drive 4.2 miles to the trailhead. Be alert for the signed trailhead. Take a sharp right down into the small parking area.

   To reach Willow Creek, start in Creede and drive 7 miles north on West Willow Creek Road (CR 503), which is 2WD the whole way, to the Equity

HISTORY: San Luis Peak in the La Garita Mountains on the western edge of the San Luis Valley borrowed its name from the valley below, the world's largest alpine desert at 8,000 square miles. No record exists of its first ascent, but Utes probably were the first to reach its summit. The Los Pinos Agency for the Tabeguache Utes was located on Cochetopa Creek northeast of the peak.

Mine. If you have a 4WD drive vehicle, continue another 1.5 miles to where the road makes a sharp left.

NORTHEAST RIDGE ROUTE: Hike west up Stewart Creek Valley, keeping to the right (north) side of the creek most of the time. The trail is easily discernable. At the end of the valley you will see a high, flattened, pyramid-shaped peak. After climbing past several gulches coming in from the left, ascend to the saddle on the northwest slope of San Luis Peak. From this point, the summit can be seen 0.2 mile away in a west-southwest direction, but this is still a long hike.

SOUTH RIDGE ROUTE: Head northeast about 1.5 miles to the intersection with the Continental Divide Trail (CDT). Go generally east on the CDT as it contours around Spring Creek Basins. When you reach the saddle at about 12,600 feet, break off to the northwest and continue about 1.3 miles up the South Ridge of San Luis Peak to the summit.

Left: San Luis Peak, looking east from the Colorado Trail.

Below: San Luis Peak, looking southwest from the Organ Mountain–San Luis Peak saddle.

SAN LUIS PEAK

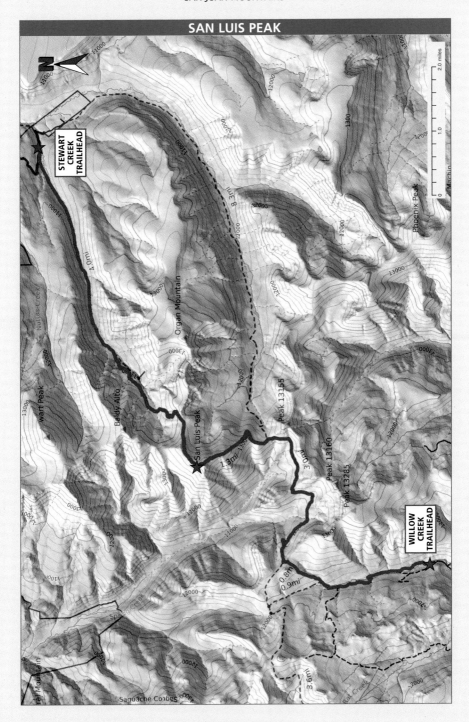

STEWART CREEK TRAILHEAD

WILLOW CREEK TRAILHEAD

San Luis Peak

Organ Mountain

Baldy Alto

Peak 13155

Peak 13160

Peak 13225

Phoenix Peak

Stewart Peak

Machin

4.0mi

8.3mi

1.3mi

3.0mi

0.8mi

0.9mi

3.6mi

Nutras Creek

Saguache Colorado

Stewart Creek

2.0 miles

1.0

0

Uncompahgre Peak 14,321 feet 6

MAPS	Trails Illustrated 141–Telluride/Silverton/Ouray/Lake City
RATING	More difficult
ELEVATION GAIN	3,000 feet
ROUND-TRIP DISTANCE	7.5 miles
ROUND-TRIP TIME	7 hours
NEAREST TOWN	Lake City
RANGER DISTRICT	US Forest Service, Gunnison Ranger District, 970-641-0471

COMMENT: Following the Nellie Creek Trail to the South Ridge is the best choice. The CFI does not recommend using the Matterhorn Creek Trailhead due to the sensitivity of the alpine environment.

CFI completed heavy trail maintenance of this route in 2009 and has maintained it annually since. CFI plans to begin a focused trail reconstruction/restoration effort here in 2019. A note about braided trails: Oftentimes, when hikers come across eroded trails, they walk next to the trail in search of a more stable and comfortable hiking surface. Unfortunately, this causes increasingly widened and braided trails (where multiple impacted trails run side by side). Practice Leave No Trace by always choosing to hike on the most impacted/eroded trail when you come across multiple parallel trails.

GETTING THERE: In Lake City, find CR 20 and drive west for about 5 miles. Turn north (right) onto the Nellie Creek Road. This road is not recommended for a passenger car because of steep switchbacks that can be slippery during wet weather. A 4WD vehicle is advisable. Park at the end of the road.

THE ROUTE: The Nellie Creek Trail is well traveled and easy to follow. It goes west to the southeast ridge of Uncompahgre, and then north up to the summit.

Left: Uncompahgre Peak.

173

HISTORY: Uncompahgre was probably first climbed by Utes. The name is a Ute word said to mean "hot water spring." The Hayden Survey named the mountain after the Uncompahgre River. A. D. Wilson and Franklin Rhoda made the first documented ascent in 1874, and found that grizzly bears had preceded them to the summit.

SIDEBAR TRAIL RIGHT-OF-WAY

The person coming downhill has the right-of-way, because it is often easier to stop and step aside when you are going uphill than it is when you are going downhill.

Uncompahgre Peak, looking east from the slopes of Matterhorn Peak.

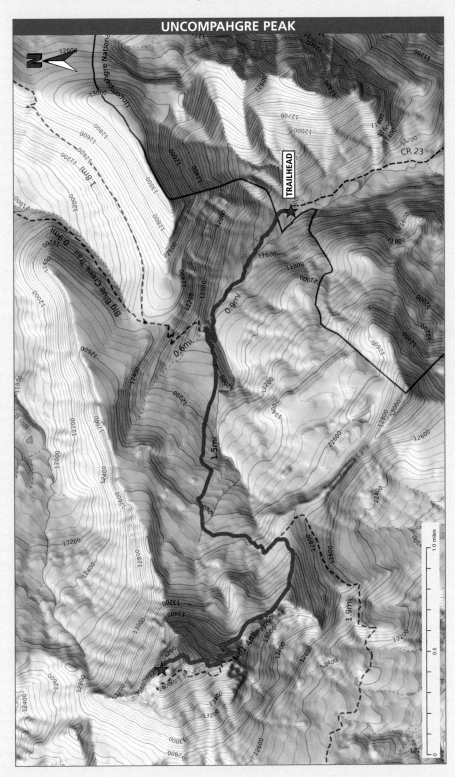

UNCOMPAHGRE PEAK

TRAILHEAD

CR 23

Uncompahgre National

Big Blue Creek Trail

1.8mi

0.9mi

0.6mi

0.9mi

1.5mi

.9mi

1.4mi

1.9mi

1.0 miles

0.5

0

Wetterhorn Peak   14,015 feet   50

MAPS	Trails Illustrated 141–Telluride/Silverton/Ouray/Lake City
RATING	More difficult
ELEVATION GAIN	3,300 feet
ROUND-TRIP DISTANCE	7 miles
ROUND-TRIP TIME	6 hours
NEAREST TOWN	Lake City
RANGER DISTRICT	US Forest Service, Gunnison Ranger District, 970-641-0471

COMMENT: There is a memorable final pitch on Wetterhorn, and all those black marks on the summit rocks are probably from lightning strikes. The Southeast Ridge via Matterhorn Creek is the standard route.

CFI completed trail construction and restoration work in 2004 and has maintained it biannually since. CFI plans to begin a focused trail reconstruction/restoration effort here in 2019.

GETTING THERE: From Lake City, go west on Henson Creek Road. Start measuring mileage from here. At 8.8 miles, there is a junction. Turn right and follow the sign for North Henson Road. At 10.8 miles, there is another junction with a sign that indicates the Matterhorn Creek trailhead is ahead. Park here if you don't have a high-clearance 4WD vehicle or turn right and continue on a rough road to the trailhead and parking area at 11.4 miles.

THE ROUTE: Hike north along the Ridgestock Driveway to the junction with the Wetterhorn Peak Trail. This junction is marked with a sign. Follow the established trail across Matterhorn Basin to the southeast summit ridgeline. Work up the ridgeline to the summit on a system of ledges. The route appears to be steep and formidable, but it goes well if the route is dry.

Left: The Souteast Face of Wetterhorn Peak.

Wetterhorn Peak, looking southeast from West Fork Pass.

HISTORY: Wetterhorn was named by Lieutenant William Marshall during the 1874 Wheeler Survey. Viewing it from nearby Uncompahgre, Marshall wrote, "The Wetterhorn… is a shark's nose…and appears inaccessible." Apparently, Marshall was familiar with the Wetterhorn in the Swiss Alps, to which he likened the Colorado peak.

SIDEBAR / WATER

We got lost and spent hours in an endless talus field on a hot day. We climbed a false summit. We ran out of water on the real summit. We were very dry when we got to the car. Carry more water than you think you will need. You have been warned.

Wetterhorn, Matterhorn, and Uncompahgre from just west of Slumgullion Pass.

WETTERHORN PEAK

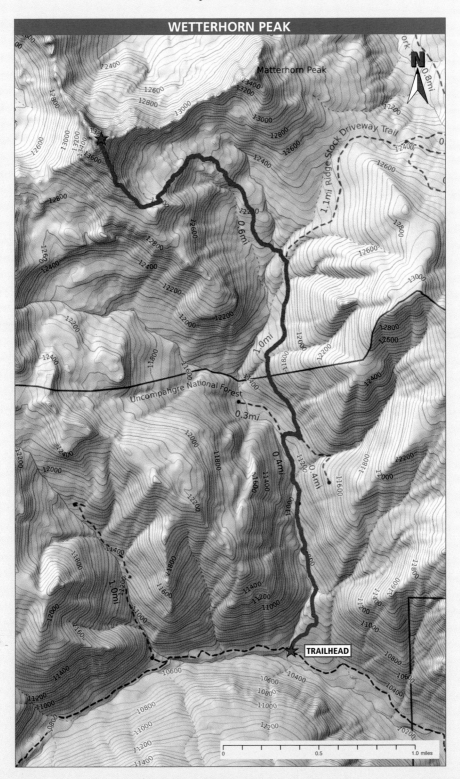

Matterhorn Peak

N
0.8mi

1.1mi Ridge Stock Driveway Trail

0.6mi

1.0mi

Uncompahgre National Forest

0.3mi

0.4mi

0.4mi

1.0mi

TRAILHEAD

0   0.5   1.0 miles

Sunset light on Redcloud
Peak, as viewed looking
northeast from Grizzly Gulch.

Redcloud Peak
Sunshine Peak

14,034 feet `46`

14,001 feet `54*`

MAPS	Trails Illustrated 141–Telluride/Silverton/Ouray/Lake City
RATING	More difficult
ELEVATION GAIN	3,700 feet to Redcloud; 4,700 feet to Sunshine
ROUND-TRIP DISTANCE	9 miles to Redcloud; 12 miles to Sunshine
ROUND-TRIP TIME	7 hours to Redcloud; 10 hours to Sunshine
NEAREST TOWN	Lake City
RANGER DISTRICT	Bureau of Land Management, Gunnison Resource Area, 970-641-0471

COMMENT: There are still a couple of years to climb the 54th highest Fourteener before it gets downgraded to a Thirteener, probably in 2022 (*see* Counting Fourteeners, page 11–14). These peaks are traditionally done together by ascending the Northeast Ridge of Redcloud, then traversing the ridge to Sunshine.

Multiple braided trails exist between Redcloud and Sunshine peaks. Try to hike on the most prominent of these trails to prevent further impacts. CFI does not recommend ascending or descending the Northwest Face of Sunshine.

GETTING THERE: From Lake City, drive approximately 15 miles up the Lake Fork of the Gunnison River on CR 30. Take the right fork onto CR 4 toward Cinnamon Pass and drive for just over 4 miles to Grizzly Creek at 10,400 feet. There is an excellent campsite near Grizzly Gulch in the area of Silver Creek with water (not potable) and an outhouse.

THE ROUTE: Using the standard cairn route, hike northeast up the trail 2 miles to the northwest side of Silver Creek. Continue on the trail along the creek. At timberline, cross the creek, gain the saddle northeast of Redcloud, and climb the ridge southwest for 1 mile to the summit.

To get to Sunshine, follow the Redcloud ridge south for 1.5 miles. You will drop 500 feet between peaks. Return over Redcloud. In the saddle between Redcloud and Sunshine there is an apparent "descent" into the South Fork drainage that looks very inviting. It is steep, dangerous, and contains tricky talus. Once you take this wrong trail, it is extremely difficult to retrace your steps back to the saddle to access the safer route.

Redcloud Peak from high in Grizzly Gulch.

HISTORY: A palette of reds, yellows, and oranges dots Redcloud's rounded slopes, and it was informally called Red Mountain. J. C. Spiller of the Wheeler Survey upgraded this name to the poetic Redcloud in 1874. Later that summer, Hayden Survey members were chased off neighboring Sunshine Peak by lightning.

Sunset reflection of Redcloud and Sunshine peaks in Burrows Park.

Sunshine Peak from Cinnamon Pass, looking east at sunset.

REDCLOUD PEAK | SUNSHINE PEAK

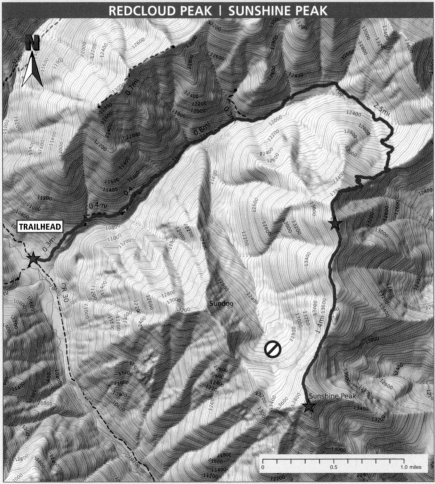

Handies Peak

14,058 feet **40**

MAPS	Trails Illustrated 141–Telluride/Silverton/Ouray/Lake City
RATING	Moderate
ELEVATION GAIN	3,600 feet for the East Slope; 2,800 feet for the Southwest Slope
ROUND-TRIP DISTANCE	8 miles for the East Slope; 7.5 miles for the Southwest Slope
ROUND-TRIP TIME	6 hours for the East Slope; 5 hours for the Southwest Slope
NEAREST TOWN	Lake City
RANGER DISTRICT	Bureau of Land Management, Gunnison Resource Area, 970-641-0471

COMMENT: There are two standard routes, the East Slope from American Basin and the Southwest Slope from Grizzly Gulch.

GETTING THERE: From Lake City, drive approximately 15 miles up the Lake Fork of the Gunnison River on CR 30. Take the right fork onto CR 4 toward Cinnamon Pass and drive for just over 4 miles to Grizzly Creek at 10,400 feet. There is an excellent campsite near Grizzly Gulch in the area of Silver Creek with water (not potable) and an outhouse.

To reach the West Slope Route, continue south on Cinnamon Pass Road for about 3.5 miles past Grizzly Creek. Take a 4WD road heading south into American Basin. Park along this road.

EAST SLOPE ROUTE: Cross the Lake Fork of the Gunnison River, and hike up the Grizzly Gulch Trail out of the valley and west to the ridge. From the ridge it is an easy climb south to the summit.

WEST SLOPE ROUTE: Follow the road as it changes into a trail and begins to climb up grassy slopes. Continue south, then east to the south ridge of Handies, then north to the summit. Return by the same route, following the trail.

Left: Handies Peak viewed from the road to Cinnamon Pass.

Handies Peak from Grizzly Gulch.

HISTORY: Despite the beauty and rich mining history surrounding this mountain, little is known of its name or first ascent. Miners likely account for both. Prominent nearby silver mines included the Bonhomme, Champion, Cracker Jack, and Tabasco, the latter on the road to Cinnamon Pass and financed by the Tabasco Meat Sauce Company. In fact, Handies was sometimes referred to as "Tabasco."

Handies Peak's reflection, looking southeast.

HANDIES PEAK

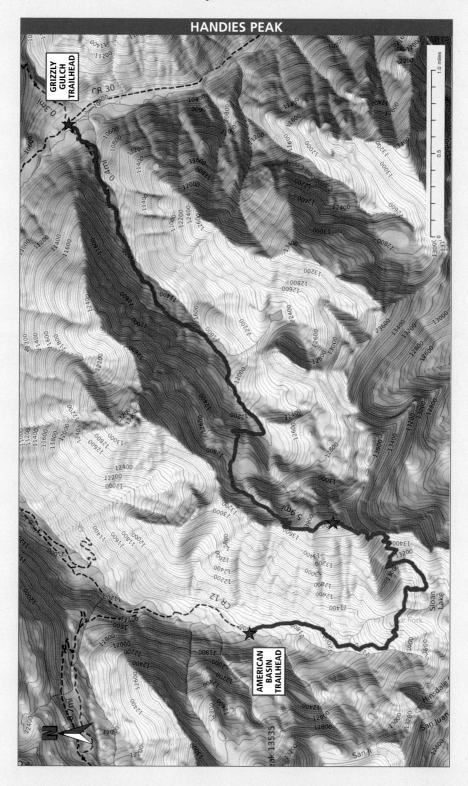

GRIZZLY GULCH TRAILHEAD

CR 30

0.3 mi

0.4 mi

S 9 mi

CR 12

AMERICAN BASIN TRAILHEAD

Sloan Lake

Lake Fork

0.7 mi

N

Peak 13535

San Ji

1.0 miles

0.5

Left to right: Windom Peak, Sunlight Spire, and Sunlight Peak at sunrise viewed from Sunlight Basin.

Sunlight Peak

14,059 feet **39**

Sunlight Spire

14,001 feet *****

Windom Peak

14,082 feet **34**

MAPS	Trails Illustrated 140–Weminuche Wilderness
RATING	Very difficult
ELEVATION GAIN	2,600 feet from camp, plus you lose and regain 1,000 feet between Sunlight and Windom
ROUND-TRIP DISTANCE	5 miles from camp
ROUND-TRIP TIME	5 hours from camp
NEAREST TOWN	Durango
RANGER DISTRICT	US Forest Service, Columbine Ranger District, 970-884-2512

COMMENT: Windom and Sunlight are close together, with 1,000 feet of elevation loss on the route connecting them. They should be climbed on the same day, unless weather dictates otherwise. Mount Eolus can also be climbed from the same high camp. Carrying a rope is a good idea. The West Ridge of Windom is the standard route, with a return to the flats and back up the South Face of Sunlight.

Some people argue that Sunlight Spire, just to the southeast, is the "59th" Fourteener. For decades, it was marked as 13,995 feet but then it got an official boost in 1991 to 14,001 feet. Because the summit obelisk requires climbing a 45-foot, 5.10 hand crack, this would be the most technically difficult of all the Fourteeners in the Lower 48 States. However, it will permanently lose Fourteener status in 2022 when it drops down to 13,999 feet (*see* Counting Fourteeners, page 11–14).

CFI completed trail construction and restoration efforts here in 2010. Please stay on existing trails, and do not cause further impacts by hiking off-trail. Due to high levels of camping use and irresponsible behavior by some campers, Chicago Basin has a high level of impact (exposed human feces and campsites that are too close to water).

GETTING THERE: To reach the trailhead, take the Durango and Silverton Railroad from Durango. Call early for reservations: 970-247-2733. When you disembark at Needleton, cross the river on the suspension bridge and backpack east 6.2 miles up the trail along Needle Creek. Camp in Chicago Basin at about 11,000 feet, in the area where the trail crosses to the south bank of Needle Creek and starts up Columbine Pass.

THE ROUTES: Follow Needle Creek and the good trail north 1 mile to Twin Lakes at 12,500 feet. Turn east up the large basin between Sunlight and Windom. Keep to the left of Peak 18 (13,472 feet), the dominant feature on the ascent. Continue east 0.2 mile and climb southeast to the west ridge of Windom at 13,250 feet, near the Peak 18–Windom Peak col, a depression in the crest of the ridge. Continue east along the ridge for 0.2 mile to the summit. Descend 1,000 feet back down to the flatlands via the ascent route, and then head northeast to pass near the saddle between Sunlight Peak and a sub-peak to its southeast. Look up at Sunlight Spire and give a sigh of relief that it isn't on the list. Head northwest to the summit, and descend via the same route.

HISTORY: Windom was named for William Windom, a senator from Minnesota and secretary of the treasury in 1881. When Hayden Survey topographer Franklin Rhoda viewed the Needle Mountains from a distance in 1874, he wrote that the range always gave his companions a feeling of uneasiness when they observed the frequent storm clouds hovering around the pointy summits.

Left to right: Sunlight Peak, Sunlight Spire, and Windom Peak viewed from Overlook Point southwest of Chicago Basin.

Windom Peak.

SUNLIGHT PEAK | SUNLIGHT SPIRE | WINDOM PEAK

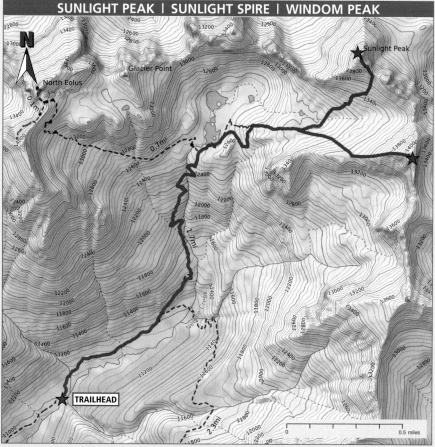

Mount Eolus
North Eolus

14,083 feet 33

14,039 feet

MAPS	Trails Illustrated 140–Weminuche Wilderness
RATING	Very difficult
ELEVATION GAIN	2,900 feet from camp
ROUND-TRIP DISTANCE	5 miles from camp
ROUND-TRIP TIME	6 hours from camp
NEAREST TOWN	Durango
RANGER DISTRICT	US Forest Service, Columbine Ranger District, 970-884-2512

COMMENT: Mount Eolus can be climbed from the same Chicago Basin high camp that you use for Windom and Sunlight. The Northeast Ridge is the standard route.

CFI completed trail construction and restoration work on this peak in 2016.

GETTING THERE: To reach the trailhead, take the Durango and Silverton Railroad from Durango. Call early for reservations: 970-247-2733. When you disembark at Needleton, cross the river on the suspension bridge and backpack east 6.2 miles up the trail along Needle Creek. Camp in Chicago Basin at about 11,000 feet, in the area where the trail crosses to the south bank of Needle Creek and starts up Columbine Pass.

THE ROUTE: From Chicago Basin, follow the trail north toward Twin Lakes. Before you get to Twin Lakes, head west. As you approach the great east face of Eolus, head northeast up a slab to the saddle between Eolus and Glacier Point at 13,700 feet. Turn west-southwest to the saddle between Eolus and North Eolus. Traverse southwest across a narrow and exposed ridge that enjoys the name "Catwalk." The ridge terminates in the east face of Eolus. Use the ledges on the face, keeping to the left and taking care to select the route to ascend to the summit. If you feel the need to bag North Eolus, just scramble on over.

Left: A reflection of Mount Eolus. PHOTO BY DAVID HITE

Mount Eolus from North Eolus.   PHOTO BY DAVID HITE

HISTORY: Franklin Rhoda's assessment during the Hayden Survey that the Needle Mountains were a "regular manufactory of storms" inspired naming the highest peak there after Aeolus, the Greek god of the winds. Prospectors soon entered the area and staked claims in Chicago Basin, most likely scaling Mount Eolus and neighboring peaks.

Mount Eolus (left) and North Eolus from the east.   PHOTO BY DAVID HITE

Sunset on Mount Eolus,
looking north from near
Overlook Point.

MOUNT EOLUS | NORTH EOLUS

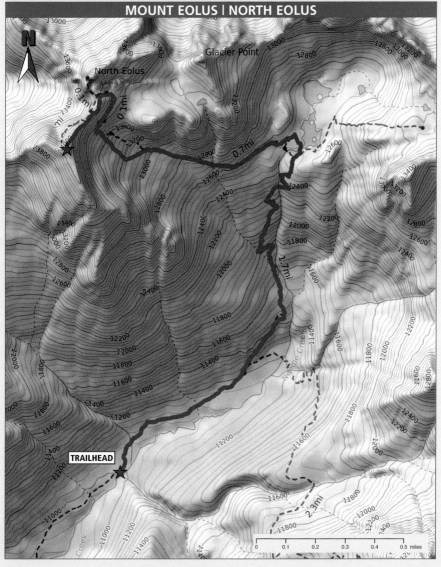

Mount Sneffels   14,150 feet   29

MAPS	Trails Illustrated 141–Telluride/Silverton/Ouray/Lake City
RATING	More difficult
ELEVATION GAIN	2,700 feet
ROUND-TRIP DISTANCE	4.5 miles
ROUND-TRIP TIME	3 to 4 hours
NEAREST TOWN	Ouray
RANGER DISTRICT	US Forest Service, Ouray Ranger District, 970-240-5300

COMMENT: A truly imposing mountain with an amazing panoramic view from the summit. The Yankee Boy Basin up toward Blue Lake Pass and then up the South Slope is the standard route.

GETTING THERE: From US 550, 0.5 mile south of Ouray, turn right onto CR 361 and drive towards Yankee Boy Basin. At 4.6 miles, CR 26 bears to the right. Continue 3 more miles to the lower 2WD trailhead at the former town of Sneffels (10,600 feet). If you have high-clearance 4WD, go right on Yankee Boy Basin Road (FR 853.1B) for 1.5 miles to the middle trailhead at 11,400 feet (shown on map). Advanced drivers with burly vehicles can reach about 12,450 feet but it probably isn't worth the stress.

THE ROUTE: Follow the Yankee Boy Basin Road up Yankee Boy Basin—famous for its alpine wildflowers and hummingbirds—to its end, then pick up the Blue Lake Pass Trail. Follow this trail to 12,600 feet, then head northeast on the trail to gain the wide Lavender Couloir. The couloir leads to a saddle at 13,500 feet. Turn northwest on the saddle and enter a narrower and steeper rock-filled couloir that leads up to the wall under the summit. Before reaching the end of this couloir, look for another much smaller and shorter couloir, and take it. It leads to the left and terminates in a V-shaped notch through which you can climb out onto the approach to the summit, about 100 yards above.

If either of these couloirs becomes too difficult because of snow, it may be possible to move to the west and approach the summit across the southwest face of Sneffels.

Left: Mount Sneffels, as viewed from the Blue Lakes Trail.

Mount Sneffels looking northwest from Black Bear Pass.

HISTORY: By most accounts, this mountain's name stems from the Hayden party's view of the peak rising above Blue Lakes Basin. Someone compared it to a dramatic scene from Jules Verne's **Journey to the Center of the Earth** and another exclaimed, "There's Snaefell!" A few insist it is from the "sniffles" suffered by many a high-altitude miner. The couloir is named for Dwight Lavender, an early mountaineer who pioneered many routes in the 1920's.

Mount Sneffels from the north.

MOUNT SNEFFELS

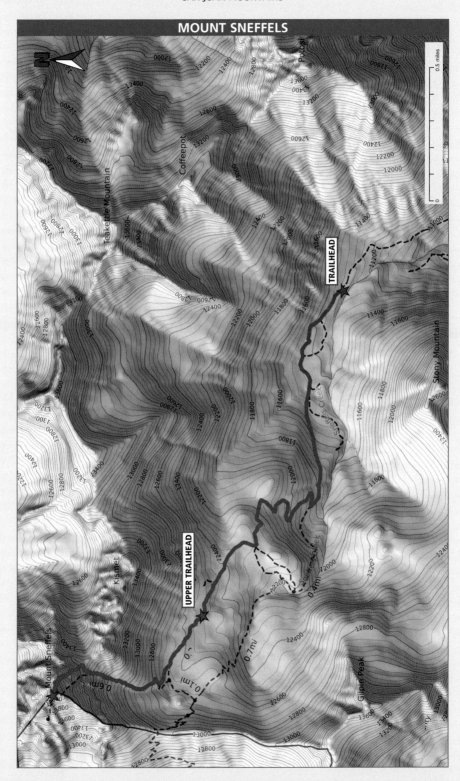

TRAILHEAD

UPPER TRAILHEAD

Mount Sneffels

Kismet

Teakettle Mountain

Coffeepot

Potosi

Stony Mountain

Gilpin Peak

Sneffels Creek

Lavender Creek

0.4mi

0.7mi

0.1mi

0.6mi

0.5 miles

Wilson Peak

14,017 feet

MAPS	Trails Illustrated 141–Telluride/Silverton/Ouray/Lake City
RATING	Very difficult
ELEVATION GAIN	3,800 feet from Silver Pick; 3,000 feet from Navajo Lake
ROUND-TRIP DISTANCE	10 miles from Silver Pick; 7 miles from Navajo Lake
ROUND-TRIP TIME	12 hours from Silver Pick; 6 hours from Navajo Lake
NEAREST TOWN	Placerville
RANGER DISTRICT	US Forest Service, Norwood Ranger District, 970-327-4261

COMMENT: The standard northern route starts in the Silver Pick Basin and goes up the Southwest Ridge. An alternative southern route approaches from Navajo Lake and ends up on the same summit ridge.

At the end of 2015, the Trust for Public Land finalized a complicated land exchange that transferred about 200 acres in Silver Pick Basin to the US Forest Service. This reestablished access to Wilson Peak via its standard Southwest Ridge route; also to Mount Wilson and El Diente via Rock of Ages saddle. CFI and the Telluride Mountain Club have been active in trail restoration on Wilson Peak.

GETTING THERE: From Placerville, drive 6.5 miles southeast on CO 145 to Vanadium. Turn right up onto Silver Pick Road (CR 60M). After 3.7 miles, when you enter the National Forest, the road becomes FR 622. Continue south for another 2.3 miles and bear right onto Elk Creek Road (FR 645), which you follow for 1.7 miles to the Wilson Mesa Trail (FR 421). Proceed another 0.5 mile to the Rock of Ages Trailhead.

SILVER PICK ROUTE: Follow the trail as it contours around to the Silver Pick Mine and then meanders south up switchbacks to the Rock of Ages saddle. From the saddle, head east and then northeast to the summit.

NAVAJO LAKE ROUTE: See the map for an alternate route from Navajo Basin. To get to Navajo Basin, follow the directions provided in the Mount Wilson section. It is a 4-mile hike, with 2,000 feet of elevation gain, to Navajo Lake. From the lake, head due east to the end of the basin and then follow the trail up northeast to the Rock of Ages Saddle. CFI plans start realignment of this trail section in 2020.

Left: Wilson Peak from the Million Dollar Highway.

Wilson Peak from the trail to Hope Lake, looking northwest.

HISTORY: Wilson Peak and its higher neighbor, Mount Wilson, were both named for A. D. Wilson, the chief topographer for the Hayden Survey, which was responsible for exploring and mapping much of the Colorado Rockies in the 1870s. Mining remains dot the peak, including the Silver Pick Mine, the largest on the mountain. This is the mountain used for the label on Coors beer.

Wilson Peak from Wilson Mesa.

Springtime view of Wilson Peak from Silver Pick Road.

WILSON PEAK

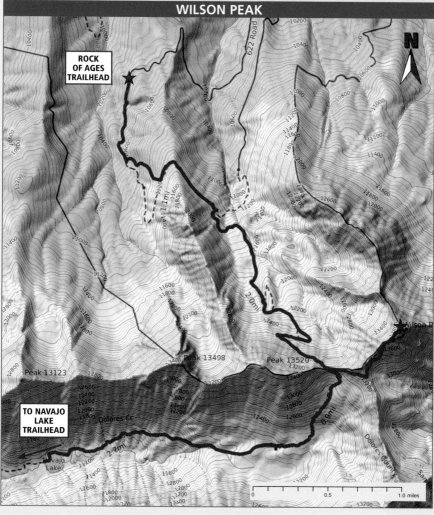

ROCK
OF AGES
TRAILHEAD

622 Road

N

Peak 13498

Peak 13520

Wilson P

Peak 13123

TO NAVAJO
LAKE
TRAILHEAD

Dolores Cr

Navajo
Lake

Dolores County

1.1 mi

2.0 mi

0.9 mi

2.7 mi

0   0.5   1.0 miles

Mount Wilson, looking west from below Ophir Pass.

Mount Wilson

14,246 feet 16

MAPS	Trails Illustrated 141–Telluride/Silverton/Ouray/Lake City
RATING	Very difficult
ELEVATION GAIN	5,200 feet from Navajo Trailhead; 3,200 feet from Navajo Lake
ROUND-TRIP DISTANCE	16 miles from Navajo Trailhead; 6.5 miles from Navajo Lake
ROUND-TRIP TIME	12 hours from Navajo Trailhead; 8 hours from Navajo Lake
NEAREST TOWN	Telluride and Rico
RANGER DISTRICT	US Forest Service, Mancos-Dolores Ranger District, 970-882-7296

COMMENT: A climbing helmet and rope are advisable for this route, and bring an ice axe early in the season. Using the Kilpacker Creek approach (see El Diente Peak), Mount Wilson and El Diente can be done in the same day by a strong party. The traverse to El Diente is about a mile long with about 500 feet of ups and downs. It isn't too difficult but only attempt it with perfect weather conditions. You can also climb Mount Wilson using the Rock of Ages Trailhead (see Wilson Peak), which will be roughly 11 miles roundtrip with 5,300 feet of elevation gain.

CFI plans to begin trail construction and restoration efforts on the Navajo Lake approach in 2020.

GETTING THERE: To approach Mount Wilson through Navajo Basin, from just north of Telluride, drive south on CO 145 for 5.5 miles beyond Lizard Head Pass. Turn right (west) on Dunton Road (FR 535). Follow Dunton Road for 6 miles, past Morgan Camp, to FR 207. Then turn right for 0.2 mile on a short road that terminates in a parking area at West Dolores River. The Navajo Lake Trailhead is located at the northern end of the parking area. Follow the trail north

HISTORY: A Hayden Survey party that included A. D. Wilson and Franklin Rhoda reached the summit of Mount Wilson via the difficult south ridge on September 13, 1874. Earlier that summer, J. C. Spiller of the Wheeler Survey had tried the route and failed. Mount Wilson remains a challenging climb from any direction.

along the river for 4 miles, and 2,000 feet of gain, to Navajo Lake, where there are campsites east of the lake. Note that campfires are prohibited in the entire Navajo Basin.

THE ROUTE: Climb east to the head of Navajo Basin. At 12,300 feet, turn south and follow the ridge on the western side between Gladstone and Mount Wilson. This should enable you to skirt the permanent snowfield along the way. At 13,800 feet, head southwest to gain the northeast ridge of Mount Wilson. At 14,100 feet, head south through a notch in the ridge. This leads to a dramatic, exposed ridge that culminates in the summit. Descend using the same route.

Rime ice-encrusted Mount Wilson, looking northwest from near Lizard Head Pass.

Sunrise on Mount Wilson, as viewed from the Hope Lake Trail.

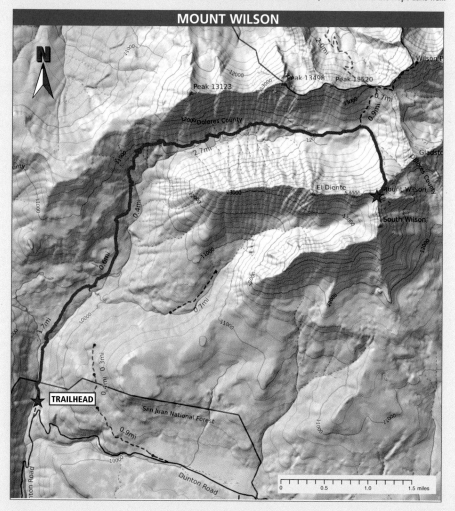

Waterfall along Kilpacker Creek and El Diente Peak.

El Diente Peak

14,159 feet

MAPS	Trails Illustrated 141–Telluride/Silverton/Ouray/Lake City
RATING	Very difficult
ELEVATION GAIN	4,100 feet
ROUND-TRIP DISTANCE	13 miles
ROUND-TRIP TIME	12 hours
NEAREST TOWN	Telluride and Rico
RANGER DISTRICT	US Forest Service, Mancos-Dolores Ranger District, 970-882-7296

COMMENT: Viewed from Kilpacker Creek, it is easy to see why this is considered its own mountain instead of just a sub-peak of Mount Wilson. It may not technically qualify since the saddle is 41 feet too high to meet the 300-foot standard but rest assured it feels like it. This is a difficult, dangerous, and challenging climb. It is strongly advised that you consult more detailed guides and carry the appropriate maps and equipment. A climbing helmet and rope are advisable for this route, and bring an ice axe early in the season. If you are up for the challenge, you can start at the Rock of Ages Trailhead.

CFI finished construction and restoration of the Kilpacker Basin approach in 2015.

GETTING THERE: From Telluride, drive south on CO 145 for 5.5 miles beyond Lizard Head Pass. Turn right (west) on Dunton Road (FR 535). After about 5.5 miles, as Dunton Road begins to lose altitude, turn right onto a small road that passes through a meadow. Continue for another 0.25 mile to a grove of trees where there is limited parking.

THE ROUTE: Hike on a closed jeep road northwest and then north and then northeast for 1.5 miles to Kilpacker Creek. Do not cross the creek. Just south of the creek, pick up a trail heading east and continue generally up along the creek after the trail crosses the creek and ends. Pass two waterfalls near timberline. Continue up the drainage to gain the Mount Wilson–El Diente ridge. Gain the ridge to the left, or west, of a formation called Organ Pipes. This route eliminates a difficult traverse around the formation. As you head for the summit, switch to the north side of the ridge.

El Diente Peak from Kilpacker Creek.

HISTORY: In 1930, Dwight Lavender, Forrest Greenfield, and Chester Price climbed the west ridge of what was then thought to be only the western sub-peak of Mount Wilson. Finding no evidence of prior visitors, they claimed a first ascent and named it El Diente, Spanish for "the tooth." Later, Lavender discovered an account of climbing Mount Wilson in August 1890 that he felt was the first ascent of El Diente.

El Diente from the southeast.   PHOTO BY DAVID HITE

El Diente from Dunton Road.

EL DIENTE PEAK

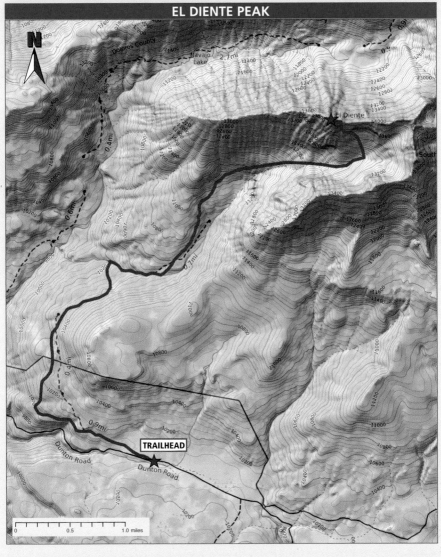

APPENDIX 1
FOURTEENERS BY HEIGHT

	MOUNTAIN	PAGE	ALTITUDE	RANGE
1	Mount Elbert	105	14,440	Sawatch
2	Mount Massive	101	14,421	Sawatch
3	Mount Harvard	125	14,421	Sawatch
4	Blanca Peak	77	14,345	Sangre de Cristo
5	La Plata Peak	109	14,336	Sawatch
6	Uncompahgre Peak	173	14,321	San Juan
7	Crestone Peak	61	14,294	Sangre de Cristo
8	Mount Lincoln	89	14,293	Mosquito
9	Castle Peak	165	14,279	Elk
10	Grays Peak	37	14,278	Front
11	Mount Antero	137	14,276	Sawatch
12	Torreys Peak	37	14,275	Front
13	Quandary Peak	85	14,271	Mosquito
14	Mount Evans	41	14,265	Front
15	Longs Peak	33	14,259	Front
16	Mount Wilson	205	14,246	San Juan
17	Mount Shavano	141	14,231	Sawatch
18	Mount Princeton	133	14,204	Sawatch
19	Mount Belford	113	14,203	Sawatch
20	Mount Yale	129	14,200	Sawatch
21	Crestone Needle	65	14,197	Sangre de Cristo
22	Mount Bross	89	14,172	Mosquito
23	Kit Carson Peak	53	14,165	Sangre de Cristo
24	Maroon Peak	153	14,163	Elk
25	Tabeguache Peak	141	14,162	Sawatch
26	Mount Oxford	113	14,160	Sawatch
27	El Diente Peak	209	14,159	San Juan

MOUNTAIN	PAGE	ALTITUDE	RANGE
28 Mount Democrat	89	14,155	Mosquito
29 Mount Sneffels	197	14,150	San Juan
30 Capitol Peak	145	14,130	Elk
31 Pikes Peak	49	14,115	Front
32 Snowmass Mountain	149	14,099	Elk
33 Mount Eolus	193	14,083	San Juan
34 Windom Peak	189	14,082	San Juan
35 Mount Columbia	125	14,077	Sawatch
36 Missouri Mountain	117	14,074	Sawatch
37 Humboldt Peak	57	14,064	Sangre de Cristo
38 Mount Bierstadt	45	14,060	Front
39 Sunlight Peak	189	14,059	San Juan
40 Handies Peak	185	14,058	San Juan
41 Culebra Peak	81	14,047	Sangre de Cristo
42 Ellingwood Point	77	14,042	Sangre de Cristo
43 Mount Lindsey	69	14,042	Sangre de Cristo
44 Little Bear Peak	73	14,037	Sangre de Cristo
45 Mount Sherman	93	14,036	Mosquito
46 Redcloud Peak	181	14,034	San Juan
47 Pyramid Peak	161	14,025	Elk
48 North Maroon Peak	157	14,019	Elk
49 Wilson Peak	201	14,017	San Juan
50 Wetterhorn Peak	177	14,015	San Juan
51 San Luis Peak	169	14,014	San Juan
52 Huron Peak	121	14,010	Sawatch
53 Mount of the Holy Cross	97	14,009	Sawatch
54 Sunshine Peak	181	14,001	San Juan

APPENDIX 2
FOURTEENERS CHECKLIST

MOUNTAIN	PAGE	CLIMBING PARTNERS	DATE
Longs Peak	33		
Grays Peak	37		
Torreys Peak	37		
Mount Evans	41		
Mount Bierstadt	45		
Pikes Peak	49		
Kit Carson Peak	53		
Humboldt Peak	57		
Crestone Peak	61		
Crestone Needle	65		
Mount Lindsey	69		
Little Bear Peak	73		
Blanca Peak	77		
Ellingwood Point	77		
Culebra Peak	81		
Quandary Peak	85		
Mount Lincoln	89		
Mount Democrat	89		
Mount Bross	89		
Mount Sherman	93		
Mount of the Holy Cross	97		
Mount Massive	101		
Mount Elbert	105		
La Plata Peak	109		
Mount Belford	113		
Mount Oxford	113		
Missouri Mountain	117		

MOUNTAIN	PAGE	CLIMBING PARTNERS	DATE
Huron Peak	121		
Mount Harvard	125		
Mount Columbia	125		
Mount Yale	129		
Mount Princeton	133		
Mount Antero	137		
Mount Shavano	141		
Tabeguache Peak	141		
Capitol Peak	145		
Snowmass Mountain	149		
Maroon Peak	153		
North Maroon Peak	157		
Pyramid Peak	161		
Castle Peak	165		
San Luis Peak	169		
Uncompahgre Peak	173		
Wetterhorn Peak	177		
Redcloud Peak	181		
Sunshine Peak	181		
Handies Peak	185		
Windom Peak	189		
Sunlight Peak	189		
Mount Eolus	193		
Mount Sneffels	197		
Wilson Peak	201		
Mount Wilson	205		
El Diente Peak	209		

Illustration by Jesse Crock

Join Today.
Adventure Tomorrow.

The Colorado Mountain Club helps you maximize living in an outdoor playground and connects you with other adventure-loving mountaineers. We summit 14ers, climb rock faces, work to protect the mountain experience, and educate generations of Coloradans.

Visit cmc.org/readerspecials
for great membership offers to our readers.